Blessings.

W9-CDP-321

FEAR NOT

Fear is something that we observe in our daily lives. It has even influenced the Church. This work is timely and of benefit to any Christian who wants to walk the biblical way. I have known Pastor Conlon for many years, and he lives what he preaches. His life and devotion to God attest to the fact that the subject matter he is dealing with is relevant for our times. I highly recommend the reading of this great work.

L. John Bueno
Executive Director (Retired) of Assemblies of God World Missions

I have had the opportunity to hear Pastor Carter Conlon speak, and each time I was impressed at how he was always able to bring the message home to the people. He was discipled by my dear friend and spiritual father, David Wilkerson. I am so thankful for the legacy of strong Bible-based preaching and ministry that Pastor Carter brings to Times Square Church.

Nicky Cruz
Nicky Cruz Outreach

Here is Carter Conlon's anti-toxic, faith-strengthening tonic for your soul's peace and, thereby, your personal health and practical ability to "do life" in an increasingly unstable world.

Jack W. Hayford
Founding Pastor of The Church On The Way, Van Nuys, California
Chancellor of The King's University, Los Angeles, California

I've had the wonderful opportunity to visit Times Square Church on Sundays when I have been in New York. I learned quickly to get there very early, as seats are packed an hour before the service. Once hearing Pastor Carter Conlon, it's easy to understand why. The church defies all explanation. Located right in the very heart of New York's Times Square/Theater District, it attracts people of all faiths, races, ethnic groups and backgrounds. They experience some of the most powerful praise and worship on earth and solid, biblical preaching from Pastor Conlon. I've been blessed every time I've been there. I hope you will be as encouraged by Pastor Conlon's new book and that it will speak to you as if you're sitting in the congregation at Times Square Church.

Mike Huckabee

Governor of Arkansas
Host of "Huckabee" (FOX News) and *New York Times* Bestselling Author
of *A Simple Government: Twelve Things We Really Need From Government*

I've attended Times Square Church for many years and never fail to hear the pure and anointed Word of God from its godly pastors. It's a great joy and a deep comfort to know that God's voice is speaking "for such a time as this" in New York City and beyond.

Eric Metaxas

New York Times Bestselling Author of *Bonhoeffer: Pastor, Martyr, Prophet, Spy*

Pastor Carter Conlon is a true man of God who lives what he preaches. He has been given a special anointing of the Holy Spirit to deliver the Word of God with straightforwardness and authority, yet with mercy and grace. When this man preaches, you know you have truly heard from God's throne.

David Wilkerson (1931–2011)

Founding Pastor, Times Square Church, New York

In these pages, Pastor Carter Conlon does far more than diagnose the malady, he provides a gospel remedy: turning fully toward Jesus. I believe that what we read here will turn our hearts to our first love.

Gary Wilkerson
World Challenge

I have known Carter Conlon for many years and have witnessed his fervent heart for Christ, his love for the alienated and the poor, and his uncompromising attention to God's Word. You may not feel comfortable with everything he says, but he will force you to think and take your calling seriously.

Dr. Ravi Zacharias
Bestselling Author and Speaker

FEAR NOT

CARTER CONLON

WITH LESLIE QUON

Regal

For more information and
special offers from Regal Books, email us at
subscribe@regalbooks.com

Published by Regal
From Gospel Light
Ventura, California, U.S.A.
www.regalbooks.com
Printed in the U.S.A.

Library of Congress Cataloging-in-Publication Data
Conlon, Carter.
Fear not / Carter Conlon, with Leslie Quon.
p. cm.
Includes bibliographical references and index.
ISBN (hard cover) 978-0-8307-6391-7 (alk. paper)
ISBN (trade paper) 978-0-8307-6561-4
1. Fear—Religious aspects—Christianity. I. Quon, Leslie. II. Title.
BV4908.5.C66 2012
241'.3—dc23
2012016004

Rights for publishing this book outside the U.S.A. or in non-English languages are
administered by Gospel Light Worldwide, an international not-for-profit ministry.
For additional information, please visit www.glww.org, email info@glww.org, or write
to Gospel Light Worldwide, 1957 Eastman Avenue, Ventura, CA 93003, U.S.A.

To order copies of this book and other Regal products in bulk quantities,
please contact us at 1-800-446-7735.

To Mom and Dad, Charles and Kay Conlon,
who gave their all to give me the best
life they thought possible. In turn, Jesus gave
you both the best He had for you. You found
Him as Lord and Savior in the
final days of your lives. Well done.

CONTENTS

ACKNOWLEDGMENTS

Special thanks to Leslie Quon for compiling, researching and editing the thoughts that the Lord has given me on this topic over the years. Your skill and dedication to this task are invaluable. Thanks also to Tammy Shannon, who has cheerfully taken on the responsibility of guiding me through the publishing process.

FOREWORD

Many psychologists and other medical professionals identify fear as our primary and most severe disease. The energy of fear can affect a person's spiritual, physical and psychological health. Its byproducts can trigger other diseases, too. Sadly, the pervasiveness of fear causes many people to hunker down in emotional and psychological bunkers, simply awaiting the next big catastrophe.

This commonplace scenario is definitely not God's plan for His people. Paul speaks with a clarion voice in 2 Timothy 1:7 when he declares, "For God has not given us a spirit of fear, but of power and of love and of a sound mind" (*NKJV*).

Many contemporary books merely encourage us to forget our own reality for a few hours. Not this one. *Fear Not* is resolute in declaring that everything that happens in our world must be seen as a component of the divine plan established before the creation of the universe. Author and Pastor Carter Conlon appeals to Christians to set aside anxious uncertainty, so that they can live with a calm assurance in the comforting guarantee that God's promises are sure. God will not fail to provide for those who put their trust in Him.

Since Pastor David Wilkerson walked through Times Square in 1986, responded to the call of God to minister in New York City, and founded Times Square Church, there has been a clear prophetic voice in that pulpit. As Wilkerson's successor, Pastor Conlon is faithfully fulfilling that same call today. What a refreshing thing to hear a prophetic voice declaring the authenticity of Holy Scripture.

Pastor Carter Conlon writes like he speaks—clearly, concisely and to the point—with no wasted words along the way. He navigates across the economic, religious and political landscape with the kind of wisdom that comes from personally living in accordance with biblical truth. He does not randomly speculate on the possibility that God's Word may be true. He unashamedly declares that the biblical narrative was meant to rule. For Pastor Conlon, truth always wins out over fitting in with cultural norms.

As president of the American Bible Society, I was especially delighted to learn that Pastor Conlon's journey from fear to faith began with a personal encounter with God's Word. A fresh hearing of the Word of God has always been central to the critical spiritual movements of the people of God.

In *Fear Not*, Pastor Conlon reminds us that the social and economic crises of our age are not due to bad luck or accident. They are unavoidable consequences of a fallen world and the misguided judgments man makes in attempting to deal with the world's problems without relying on God. The solutions to a fallen world will not come from the wisdom of the world. Our solutions are within the heart of God. We must be near Him to hear Him. Failure to hear and obey the voice of the Lord is the spring from which all fears emerge.

In Mark 4:38 Jesus compared the fear of the disciples to a lack of faith. When they thought their boat was going to sink, the disciples asked, "Teacher, do You not care that we are perishing?" (*NKJV*). Jesus responded, "Why are you so fearful? How is it that you have no faith?" (v. 40, *NKJV*).

The only hope for a legitimate appraisal of our situation and for real change is to seek a reference point outside of the fallen world order. Pastor Conlon assures us that God stands ready to meet us, even in the face of coming storms, to give us peace and hope. God reminds us in Isaiah 41:10: "Fear not, for I am with you; be not dismayed, for I am your God. I will strengthen you, yes, I will help you, I will uphold you with My righteous right hand" (*NKJV*).

Lamar Vest
President and CEO, American Bible Society

LETTER TO PASTOR CARTER
FROM LEONARD RAVENHILL

December 15, 1990

Beloved Carter,

I am jealous over you with a godly jealousy. I pray you may know the glory of God and speak with endowment our age has not known, with the "utterance" St. Paul speaks of in Ephesians 6:19, with the wisdom and fire of our Holy Father. That you and I may be able to say "the prince of this world cometh and findeth nothing in me" [see John 14:30]. No pride! No itch for recognition, no place of pre-eminence desired. Just the opportunity to reflect His mercy, peace and love. The calling we have is awesome. As He was so are we in *this* world—now! God keep us free from any smudges, stain or schemes of this world.

I pray that each service will be so charged with God that ineradicable truths will be engraved on *young* hearts as you speak. "Fire begets fire" and vision [begets] vision, and zeal [begets] zeal. . . .

The Lord whom ye seek shall suddenly come to His temple.

Blessings,
Brother Leonard Ravenhill
Author and Evangelist (1907–1994)

FEAR NOT

PREFACE

The nurse dropped the blood pressure cuff and ran out of the room. Apparently she feared that the young man who had just been rushed in by ambulance was in grave danger of an immediate stroke or heart attack. He clearly had a problem, but the source wasn't physical; rather, it was spiritual and emotional. Lying there in the hospital was an otherwise healthy human being, not yet 20 years old—a victim of *fear*.

I recall the scene so vividly because that young man was me. This wasn't my first visit to the emergency room; I had been there in the past for the same reason. Today we call these episodes panic attacks—the result of an interior implosion, somewhat like a computer meltdown due to overload, only striking a human body. Without warning, the walls seem to start closing in. It feels as if somebody is pouring a bucket of sand on your head while insidiously declaring the eternal hopelessness of your situation. The nonstop ringing in your ears is deafening, and it seems like your heart is going to pound right out of your chest. Surely death is right at the door!

I started having these panic attacks when I was only 15. Perhaps it was because of the high expectations I placed on myself and that others placed on me as well, all of which I felt powerless to fulfill. All I know is that without warning, fear became my constant companion. It got so bad that I would sometimes be afraid to travel too far from home or spend a night by myself, even in familiar surroundings.

The first time I collapsed in class was during my last year of high school. It was a repeat year, which only served to further my sense of hopelessness. My parents were good people who wanted only the best for me. Because they had both been denied an education, they in turn instilled in me many dreams that a war and subsequent circumstances had prevented them from attaining. I eventually embraced their idea that a university education was essential in order to be successful, without which I would be regarded as a failure. The only problem was that I had always hated school.

I ended up going to university essentially to please my mom and dad. By this time, however, fear had gained a tight grip on me. Pills and tranquilizers were part of my daily routine, and I attended most of my classes so drugged that I felt as if I were underwater. The classes I dreaded the most were the ones with only a few students, increasing the chances that I would be singled out. If I was called on, there were usually only two options: flee the room or pass out from fear.

I eventually reached the point where I was afraid of fear itself. Imagine the embarrassment of having everyone turn their attention toward you, only to have them watch as you begin to panic and sweat profusely, frantically looking around for a way to escape. I know what it's like to feel literally trapped by fear.

In fairness, there were times when fear would seem to leave me alone. When I was in a social setting without walls, or when I was among family and friends I trusted, I often experienced periods of relief. In the midst of it all, however, I felt a nagging doubt that I would ever be truly free and that sudden bouts of fear were destined to be my lifetime companions. I grew angry about my inescapable situation and, sadly, often took it out on those closest to me.

Shortly after graduating from university in 1975, I became a member of a city police department. By this time, I had found one way to essentially control the fear: keep my body in a state of semi-exhaustion. I would work out daily at a local gym in addition to running a couple of miles most nights. I wasn't completely free of fear, but at least it seemed to be more manageable. Unfortunately, I also began to drink quite heavily, to the point where several of my friends grew rather concerned. You see, fear never really lets you go. It just drives you into deeper practices while giving the illusion that your own efforts are finally conquering it.

It was in early 1978 that I began to think about God. I didn't really know why these thoughts suddenly began to arise in my mind, for I hadn't been a person with much concern for spiritual things up to this point. (I later learned that God had actually put it on the hearts of three Charismatic Catholic ladies to pray for me—a young police officer whom they barely knew! They later recounted how the Lord had told them that He was going to use my life in a significant way for His purposes.) One day I even found myself talking to God, saying something along the lines of, "God, if You are out there and not just part of some unreachable religious thing that people do, I wouldn't mind knowing who You are." Not much of a prayer, but I now know that God heard it.

Through a series of events, a Christian police officer began to share his faith with me, and for the first time in my life, I heard that God had sent His Son, Jesus Christ, to die on a cross to pay the penalty for all the wrong I had done. Among the many things he shared was the promise written in the New Testament: "If any man be in Christ, he is a new creature: old things are passed away; behold, all things are become new" (2 Cor. 5:17). How incredible this promise seemed! Not only could I have eternal life in heaven with God but also a new life while still here on this earth! It seemed too good to be true.

Inspired to try reading the Bible for myself, I began in the Gospel of John, asking Jesus to help me understand it. When I had finished, I found myself confronted with a decision: If Jesus offered eternal and abundant life, and if He was the only way to salvation, then He required a full surrender of my life to Him. I came to the conclusion that it was all or nothing.

On May 12, 1978, I pulled my car over to the side of the road and said a simple prayer that went something like this: "Jesus, if what my friend has told me is true, then I invite You into my life and ask You to be my Lord and Savior." I then went to work my shift as usual with no seeming change that night.

It was the next morning that I knew something had happened. When I awoke, I literally felt different. Something inside of me had changed.

I began to avidly read the Bible with an inner assurance that this was the Word of God and that it could be trusted. Each scriptural promise was like a cup of cool water to a starving and thirsty man. Truth began to penetrate my heart so deeply that tears would often flow freely while I read.

Yet not too long after these days of newness and re-freshing, my old enemy of fear tried to remind me that it hadn't lost control of my life. One night, my wife and I were just falling asleep when suddenly the old symptoms of fear decided to pay me a visit once again. I got out of bed and went downstairs to the living room. Suddenly the walls started closing in, and I experienced the familiar ringing in my ears. The old hellish voices, now accompanied by laughter, taunted me that my new-found faith was somehow a fraud. However, I had been reading my Bible that week, and one promise in particular had made an imprint on my mind. The apostle Paul wrote these incredible words recorded in Romans 8:31: "If God be for us, who can be against us?" It was on the strength of this one statement that I stood my ground.

I remember the words that suddenly came out of my mouth: "Satan, you can only kill me if God allows you to, and if He does, I am going to heaven. Either way, I win. So you throw at me all that you have, but I now throw back at you what God Himself has given me. IN THE NAME OF JESUS, THE SON OF GOD, I RESIST YOU!"

As I stood there, a white-hot fire seemed to touch my feet and progress upward through my body, finally consuming me to the top of my head. I was set free—nine years of hell on earth ended! That was more than

30 years ago, and I have never had a panic attack since. I now pastor a church of more than 8,000 people and have traveled throughout much of the world, speaking to audiences that have sometimes numbered in the hundreds of thousands.

I have learned how to fight against fear, and now it no longer has mastery over me. In the pages to come, I have done my best to convey to you the biblical truths that will keep you from succumbing to fear, especially in the troubling times in which we now live. My hope is that you and I will finish this life's journey with the same confidence that must have filled Isaac's heart when he heard these words from the mouth of God: "*Fear not*, for I am with thee, and will bless thee" (Gen. 26:24, emphasis added).

FEAR NOT

1

A COMING STORM

*But now he hath promised, saying, Yet once more
I shake not the earth only, but also heaven. And this word,
yet once more, signifieth the removing of those things
that are shaken, as of things that are made, that those
things which cannot be shaken may remain.*

HEBREWS 12:26-27

We live in a day when there are countless reasons to give in to fear. World economies teeter on the edge of meltdown in a way that most of us never dreamed we would experience in our lifetime. Fear of future provision and stability dominate much of the public media, as well as our own inward thoughts: *How will I get through tomorrow? Will I be able to keep my job? Will I have food for my family?*

We face terrifying prospects of war involving weapons of mass destruction, with seemingly no resolution. We delude ourselves by thinking that somehow we are different from those who have gone before us—that we can possess these weapons and operate them with restraint. But, of course, you and I know that's a fallacy.

From day to day, we are inundated with statistics about the perilous deterioration of our planet in the form of a potential shortage of energy supplies and food. The occurrence of natural disasters has escalated worldwide. We are even facing the breakdown of the family—the nucleus of divine order that God established in the earth to bring about stability, nurturance and order in the home and in the nation.

Everywhere we look we see the constant erosion of natural love and an increase in random and senseless acts of violence. No place is safe anymore—no school, college, gathering or church. We are living in a time when people are inwardly exploding. What a tragedy that we have raised a young generation with the message that there is no God; we have taken prayer out of the schools and refuse to teach the Word of God in our curriculum. Instead, this generation has been brought up listening to violent music and sitting in front of digital images of countless acts of violence—and then we wonder why they act out. Why are we so shocked that they have become exactly what we have taught them to be?

Add to all of this the mockery of Christ and His church. There is a nonstop push in society to cast off all godly restraint while denigrating the truly godly as narrow, bigoted, out of touch and unworthy of any serious consideration. At times, they even go so far as to consider the Christian church the source of all the problems in our world today.

WHAT IS YET TO COME

I don't believe I need to convince you that the days ahead are going to be more difficult than ever—you already know it. Something inside your heart perceives it, in spite of the deepest optimism that many try to generate. There is an underlying sense among people at every level in this society that we are about to face a storm such as we have never known before. Everything that can be shaken is about to be shaken, and I do not know if any of us can even adequately describe what is to come.

Although the world's culture is quickly spinning into something that is out of our control, we can be thankful that it is never out of God's control. In fact, He has already spoken and warned us of these very things. Jesus' disciples once asked Him, "And what shall be the sign of thy coming, and of the end of the world?" (Matt. 24:3). In other words, what will society look like? What can we expect? What will be happening in the world?

> And Jesus answered and said unto them, Take heed that no man deceive you. For many shall come in my name, saying, I am Christ; and shall deceive many. And ye shall hear of wars and rumors of wars: see that ye be not troubled: for all these things must come to pass, but the end is not yet. For nation shall rise against nation, and kingdom against kingdom: and there shall be famines, and pestilences, and earthquakes, in divers places. All these are the beginning of sorrows. Then shall they deliver you up to be afflicted, and shall kill you: and ye shall be hated

of all nations for my name's sake. And then shall many be offended, and shall betray one another, and shall hate one another. And many false prophets shall rise, and shall deceive many (Matt. 24:4-11).

Not only did Jesus foretell the wars, earthquakes, famines and outbreaks of disease that are unfolding before our eyes, but He also warned us that in the last days, religious deception will reach epic proportions. In fact, the end-time strategy of Satan is clear: Divert those who are trying to find refuge during calamitous times by presenting a myriad of false Christ-options along the way.

It is actually quite a clever military strategy. Satan himself is the author of much of the chaos in the world, and when the chaos begins to mount, he will put false signposts throughout the world that claim to point the way to Christ. Many will be trying to find refuge in the kingdom of God, rushing to find the ark of safety. But they will be inundated with signs everywhere that say Jesus is this way; Jesus is over there; this is the way to life; that is the way to safety. Jesus warned us, "Wherefore if they shall say unto you, Behold, he is in the desert; go not forth: behold, he is in the secret chambers; believe it not" (Matt. 24:26).

This religious deception will be aimed at the professing church of Jesus Christ—at the casual believer and the sincere believer alike. The deception is actually already here, but it will intensify in the coming days. Satan's goal will be to confuse the people of God—to confuse the prodigals who are trying to come home to the safety of the presence of the Lord. There will be an increase of voices claiming to speak for God that will lead many people astray.

Jesus said, "And because iniquity shall abound, the love of many shall wax cold" (Matt. 24:12). Many will be led astray by false voices, but others will give up the race simply because they are overcome by the magnitude of what they are up against.

There will be a greater outbreak of lawlessness, as we are already beginning to see in the Western world today. What is happening is appalling—the way people live, the words they speak, what is coming across in the media. We are going to witness this continued moral slide in society, and what is going to happen will shock people—especially those who are godly. Iniquity will abound, and many people will simply give up because it will all seem to be too hard. Society will appear to be pushing with too much force in the opposite direction, and there will be so few who will be willing to listen to the gospel.

AND WITHIN WERE FEARS

Perhaps at this point you cannot even fathom dealing with the peril ahead because you are consumed with your own personal trial. It may even be the fear of something that God is calling you to do. However, the Scriptures bear witness that the battles we face are common to all men. There is no temptation that is unique to you, including the temptation to give in to fear.

I remember when the Lord called me to leave my secure employment, my retirement plan, everything I had accumulated and worked for—all in order to pastor a group of 17 people who were meeting in a hotel. It was insane in the natural, yet I knew that God was leading me to do it. I clearly remember having to fight through the fears. What about my children? What about their education? Will I really be able to fulfill all that God has called me to be?

Even the apostle Paul expressed this common struggle when he said, "For, when we were come into Macedonia, our flesh had no rest, but we were troubled on every side; without were fightings, within were fears" (2 Cor. 7:5). Paul was saying, "Listen, I had to fight fear. I came up against furious opposition with things seen and unseen. There were times when I could identify the opposition, yet there were other times when it just seemed as if hell with all its fury was fighting against me."

When Paul said, "without were fightings and within were fears," he was referring to those fears that are common to all men: *Can I get through this? Do I have the strength to keep going? What if I fail?* Although the temptation to be fearful was constantly knocking on the door of Paul's heart, we see in the Scriptures that he refused to draw back from what God was calling him to do. Even when he was warned that there would be tribulation and afflictions awaiting him, he was able to assert, "But none of these things move me, neither count I my life dear unto myself, so that I might finish my course with joy, and the ministry, which I have received of the Lord Jesus, to testify the gospel of the grace of God" (Acts 20:24).

Yes, you may have a deep sense of foreboding today because of world events and society's depravity. For those who are without God, indeed there is a legitimate reason to be fearful. But for those who know God, what the world sees as catastrophe, we will be able to embrace in some measure as an opportunity for God to give us His grace to endure. It will be a grace not just to walk through it, barely making it to the end, but rather grace to take full advantage of the tremendous opportunity for men and women to hear the gospel of Jesus Christ.

So prepare yourself now. This is the time to get spiritually ready to face whatever is going to happen in the coming days. The world is quickly unraveling, and things will continue to degenerate. Every person in Christ will face opposition from within and from without. Yet, in the midst of it all, we must be able to hear the word of the Lord to His church: *"Fear not."*

FEAR NOT

2

LIVING IN FEAR
WHERE NO FEAR IS

The fool hath said in his heart, There is no God.
Corrupt are they, and have done abominable iniquity:
there is none that doeth good. God looked down from heaven
upon the children of men, to see if there were any that did
understand, that did seek God. Every one of them is gone
back . . . there is none that doeth good. . . . Have the workers
of iniquity no knowledge? who eat up my people as they eat
bread: they have not called upon God. There were they in
great fear, where no fear was: for God hath scattered the
bones of him that encampeth against thee.

PSALM 53:1-5

L iving in fear is paralyzing. You can become so gripped by fear's hold that you are no longer able to function as a normal human being. That was the story of my life before I was delivered from panic attacks. I constantly had to avoid settings that would make me apprehensive, which often precluded me from being able to fully enjoy social interactions that most anyone else would. If I were speaking with someone at a gathering, I would be simultaneously scanning the room for the nearest exit, always aware of the need to strategically position myself for a quick escape if necessary. I simply could not sit in a room and relax.

Of course, I later learned that you do not have to live in any kind of fear if you are a Christian. The Lord clearly promises to cover His own people—to walk with them through the flood and through the fire (see Isa. 43:2). He reminds us in His Word that the children of God are safe in the Father's hand where nobody can snatch them out (see John 10:28-29). He has given us the testimonies and witness of Scripture to banish fear's grip. As Paul said, "[I] am persuaded that he is able to keep that which I have committed unto him against that day" (2 Tim. 1:12).

So why, then, are so many of God's servants still feeling the effects of fear today? It is as if, as the psalmist

David put it, "There were they in great fear, where no fear was" (Ps. 53:5).

Notice that David began this psalm by saying, "The fool hath said in his heart, There is no God" (Ps. 53:1). This is an incredible statement—one that is more complex than it appears on the surface. As you consider this verse, your initial thought may be of the person who makes such a declaration against the existence of God. Ironically, this person argues that the very God who gave him the power to reason does not exist. However, according to Romans 1:20-22, there is a declaration in nature itself that points to the existence of God. This means that everybody will one day stand before the Lord without excuse. People of every nation, culture and language have an opportunity through the witness of the heavens themselves—by the very majesty and clockwork of the universe—to know that there is a sovereign God. Yet, in the midst of all this, men and women who have been given the breath of life by God are still declaring that there is no God.

The ultimate tragedy of such fools is that one day they will stand before the throne of God and finally, for a brief moment, understand the love of the One who created them—a love so immeasurable, so pure, so far beyond anything you or I can even now fathom—only to be put out of the presence of that love for all eternity.

I think also of the one who mentally fashions a god who will not hold him accountable for wrong, refusing to believe there is a God who has the right to govern his life. Have you ever noticed that fallen humanity desires to create its own god? While Moses was up on the mountain, meeting with the Lord and preparing to bring the revelation of God to that particular generation, the Israelites became impatient and insisted that Aaron make gods to go before them. So Aaron collected gold earrings from the people, threw them into a fire and fashioned a cow. When the people saw it, they declared, "These are the gods who brought us out of Egypt. Let's hold a party now to our cow, and let's worship this thing!" (see Exod. 32:4). Something in the heart of mankind wants to form his own god—the kind of god that he would like to serve.

However, God has a standard of right and wrong, and those who belong to Him willingly embrace this truth. Rather than trying to mold God to fit their image, they allow the Holy Spirit to mold them into the image of God.

Those who are in Christ embrace the changes that God brings into their life. People who were once thieves begin to work and make an honest living; liars begin to speak truth; the unmerciful find the mercy of God not only extended to them, but through them. Selfish people become compassionate, freely giving of themselves and of the resources God has provided in order to meet the needs of others. They are changed by the power of the Holy Spirit into the very image of the Christ who lives within them.

Over the years, the Lord changed me from being a self-focused man into someone who genuinely cares for others. He taught me what it means to begin to love my wife as Christ loves the Church (see Eph. 5:25). He gave me the desire to be a good father and to learn how to serve my family. It was the Lord who did these things in and through my life. And this I know not by my testimony, but by the testimony of those closest to me.

A changed life is the irrefutable evidence that one has been born again by the Spirit of God. If there is no change—if a person continually tries to make God fit his own image—he is deceived. He is living in a fool's paradise with no true salvation.

David wrote, "God looked down from heaven upon the children of men, to see if there were any that did understand, that did seek God" (Ps. 53:2). It is as if the Lord is looking down on the earth, asking, "Who is willing to come into My presence? Who is willing to be conformed to My image? Who is willing to believe My Word rather than bowing to fear in this evil generation?"

WHOSE CAMP WILL BE TREMBLING?

In the life of David, we find an example of someone who was willing to believe God in the face of overwhelming odds. Could it be that David was looking back in retrospect when he wrote, "There were they in great fear, where no fear was: for God hath scattered the bones of him that encampeth against thee: thou hast put them to shame, because God hath despised them" (Ps. 53:5)? Perhaps he had a vivid memory of the day he walked into the camp of the Israelite army as a young boy, sent by his father with a bit of cheese and some bread to go check on his brothers.

> It was the time when the Philistines were encamped against Israel on the other side of a great valley, and every morning and evening for 40 days a giant named Goliath stood up to challenge the armies of Israel: "Choose you a man for you, and let him come down to me. If he be able to fight with me, and to kill me, then will we be your servants: but if I prevail against him, and kill him, then shall ye be our servants, and serve us" (1 Sam. 17:8-9).

King Saul and all the armies of Israel simply stood around trembling, unable to fight. How often does the devil do the very same thing to us today—roaring across the valley and straight into our lives, leaving us trembling? We are living in a generation with giants on every side, filth and perversion surrounding us. Confusion seems to reign, many times even in the camp of God's people, with a host of giants claiming they have the power to eradicate the testimony of Jesus Christ. It is causing a trembling in the camp—even in the hearts of Christ's followers.

Remember, God is more powerful than any enemy that will ever come against you. He is more powerful than any struggle or fear you will ever have to face. However, when you magnify your enemies above the greatness of your God, you are saying in your heart, just as the fool, "There is no God." That is exactly what King Saul and the Israelites were doing. They were looking down at this loud-mouthed giant on the other side of the valley, and in their hearts they were saying, "There is no God."

In reality, it should have been the devil's camp trembling. Recall that when Joshua sent the two Israelites to spy out Jericho, the prostitute Rahab said to them, "I know that the LORD hath given you the land, and that your terror is fallen upon us, and that all the inhabitants of the land faint because of you" (Josh. 2:9). The people of Jericho had heard what the Lord did to deliver the Israelites from Egypt and defeat the kings of the Amorites: "And as soon as we had heard these things, our hearts did melt, neither did there remain any more courage in any man, because of you: for the LORD your God, he is God in heaven above, and in earth beneath" (Josh. 2:11).

Yet this time, with Goliath standing before them, it was the people of God who were trembling. David described them as being "in great fear, where no fear was" (Ps. 53:5).

Picture this young boy, David, suddenly coming into the camp, leading a donkey and carrying some bread and cheese. Nobody would ever imagine that this could be God's answer to Israel's dilemma! Yet young David was someone who knew God and walked with Him. So straight into the middle of the camp he went, cheerfully greeting his brothers. I imagine he was met with words along the line of, "Thanks, kid, now head home before you get yourself hurt."

When David heard the threats of Goliath, he essentially asked, "Why is everybody afraid? This arrogant, raucous giant is attacking the integrity of God. Doesn't anyone see this? Is there not a cause?"

The Israelites instantly became annoyed because he was actually exposing their bankrupt spirituality.

Imagine all the soldiers clad with full armor, helmets, swords—convicted to the core as this young boy boldly announces, "I'll go fight him!"

Even David's older brother Eliab accused him, "Why have you come down? And with whom have you left those few sheep in the wilderness? I know your insolence and the wickedness of your heart; for you have come down in order to see the battle" (1 Sam. 17:28, *NASB*). Eliab was the oldest son of Jesse, the one whom Samuel initially thought was the Lord's anointed until God reminded him not to judge by appearance, for God looks at the heart. Now Eliab was accusing David of the very things that rendered him ineffective in the battle.

Those who have stopped short of what God has called them to be will always try to stop you when you step up to fight the battle. You will have to make your way through accusing voices—the voice of fear in your own heart as well as the devil himself coming against you. "What have you accomplished? What have you ever done to make such a boast? You have only been a keeper of a few sheep. You have only shared your testimony three times. Do you really think that is enough to stand against what is coming in society?"

Even Saul said to David, "You are not able to go against this Philistine to fight with him; for you are but a youth while he has been a warrior from his youth" (1 Sam. 17:33, *NASB*). We, too, are young in comparison to Satan, who has had an untold length of time to develop his strategy. We are no match for him in the natural.

No matter how many voices accused him, David insisted on going to fight the giant, for he knew a great truth, as he penned in Psalm 53:5: "God has scattered the bones of him who encamps against you; You have put them to shame" (*NKJV*). It takes a man who knows His God to say confidently, as David said to Goliath, "Thou comest to me with a sword, and with a spear, and with a shield: but I come to thee in the name of the LORD of hosts, the God of the armies of Israel, whom thou hast defied" (1 Sam. 17:45).

David was not moved by the threats of the enemy or the voices around him. He knew that God had already scattered the bones of those encamped against him. It was already accomplished.

THERE *IS* A GOD

While the armies of Israel stood paralyzed by unbelief and fear that day, David went into the battle with a heart full of faith, declaring, "This day the LORD will deliver you into my hand, and I will strike you and take your head from you. And this day I will give the carcasses of the camp of the Philistines to the birds of the air and the wild beasts of the earth, that all the earth may know that there is a God in Israel" (1 Sam. 17:46, *NKJV*).

David believed there was a God and that the Philistine army was already defeated. Before he stepped into the battle, he already saw Goliath dead. He saw Goliath's head severed from his body, the hosts of the armies of the Philistines scattered about and vultures eating them. David saw it all beforehand, and so he pursued in faith until it was fulfilled. Once the Philistines saw that their champion was dead, they all fled.

And so it is time to ask: What do *you* say about God? What do you say, not merely as an empty confession of words, but deep within your heart? What is He able to do for you? Will God have a testimony in you in this last hour—in a time when people around you are foolish enough to say, "There is no God"? Or will you remain in great fear where no fear is?

FEAR NOT

3

FEAR:
A POWERFUL
WEAPON

We be not able to go up against the people; for they are stronger than we. . . . We saw the giants, the sons of Anak, which come of the giants: and we were in our own sight as grasshoppers, and so we were in their sight.

NUMBERS 13:31,33

Fear is one of the most powerful weapons that Satan uses against us. In fact, the devil is the author of fear. By definition, fear is anticipation that we may suffer harm or that things might go wrong. Fear often gives way to dismay, which is discouragement. Fear arises in our hearts when something of strength superior to our own opposes us, and dismay comes when we consider our own resources. We look inside ourselves and come to the wrong conclusion that, even with Christ within us, we are not strong enough to fight the battle in front of us. That is how fear and dismay work together.

The devil's tactic is to convince us that the evil around us is going to overpower us. In fact, Satan often wins many battles without even having to face any opposition from us because we have already given in to fear and dismay. We have already run from the battle; we have fled from any place of personal difficulty and avoided the will of God. However, it is important to remember the reality of the situation: None of these threats, nor any evil, can conquer us, no matter how intimidating the situation looks.

Let me give you an example. For many years, I lived on a farm. In the barn lived a bunch of cats, and once in a while, I would see something rather humorous. The mother cat would corral a mouse out in the field and play with it until the mouse was exhausted and had no power left. She would then take the mouse to her kittens and lay it down, intending to teach the kittens how to conquer it. The humor of it all was that the mouse would stand up on its hind feet, bring its little claws out and show its slimy yellow teeth. Then it would try to make a ferocious sound, hoping that the kittens would not realize what they were dealing with. The only thing that could keep the kittens from taking the victory was if the mouse convinced them that it was something other than what it was. The kittens didn't have to fight to procure the victory. It had been laid at their feet.

We are like those kittens. Jesus has already won the victory for us. The devil really has no power to stop the work of God in our lives; his reign and all his power were cancelled on Calvary. There is nothing he can do but stand on the shore and watch the people of God go through the seas of impossibility into every promise given in Christ Jesus. The only potential power the devil has is when he can get us to agree with his reasoning and embrace his threats by concluding, "I don't think I can make it."

PARALYZED BY FEAR

This is exactly what happened to the children of Israel as recorded in the book of Numbers. They had been miraculously delivered from Egypt and had finally come to the border of Canaan. They were just about to possess a land flowing with milk and honey—all that God had promised to give them—only to be paralyzed by fear. When we get to the throne of God one day, I wonder how many people will realize they had arrived at that exact same place—right to the edge of all that God had intended for them to possess.

When Moses sent the 12 spies into the Promised Land, they returned with the report that it was indeed a land flowing with milk and honey, just as God said it was. Similarly, if I were to ask you today if the Bible is true, you would most likely assert, "Yes, it is true. Everything that God says is the truth." You have no debate with that, and neither did the children of Israel when they came to the border. They said the land was exactly as God had described.

Despite this assurance, all but two of the spies focused on the giants in the land: "We be not able to go up against the people; for they are stronger than we. . . . The land, through which we have gone to search it, is a land that eateth up the inhabitants thereof; and all the people that we saw in it are men of a great stature. And there we saw the giants, the sons of Anak, which come of the giants: and we were in our own sight as grasshoppers, and so we were in their sight" (Num. 13:31-33). All they could see was the opposition there—things bigger and stronger than they were, which caused them to look to their own strength in dismay. In the same way, we often conclude, "I can't do it. It's true, but not for me."

That's fear talking! It is how the devil always operates. God sets before us something impossible—a life where His promises are true, where we walk in His power, where healing flows through our lives, where we are able to win a society bent on rebellion to the things of God. He assures us with His promise to keep and guide us to fulfillment of His Word. All the while, the enemy attempts to get us to look inward at our own frailty and tells us it cannot be done. He hopes we will shrink back in fear.

We must settle the fact that there will always be competing voices in our ears—the voice of God with His promises to us, and the voice of the enemy, magnifying the opposition and our own frailties. A true word was given to the children of Israel through Joshua and Caleb, but it was accompanied by a false word as well—an alternate view, a secondary assessment of the difficulty that had come to their doorstep. It was up to the people to choose which word they were going to believe.

Unfortunately, as so often happens in the face of fear, the children of Israel succumbed to the louder voice—not to the voice of truth, not to the voice speaking for God, but to the one in their hearts and ears that was louder at that moment. "And all the congregation lifted up their voice, and cried; and the people wept that night" (Num. 14:1). Fear gave way to dismay. The giants were there, the Israelites did not have the resources to fight, and they concluded they were destined for defeat. So they cried all night.

Perhaps you have found yourself in a similar situation—crying at night and waking up brokenhearted, wondering how you will face the coming days or even get out of your current personal storm. You thought that if you tried hard enough, you would be able to overcome the fear mounting inside. But suddenly you begin to realize that the more you try, the louder the voices that oppose you.

While the other 10 spies shrank back at the sight of the opposition, Joshua and Caleb chose to believe the report of the Lord, exhorting the children of Israel, "The land, which we passed through to search it, is an exceeding good land. If the LORD delight in us, then he will bring us into this land, and give it us; a land which floweth with milk and honey. Only rebel not ye against the LORD, neither fear ye the people of the land; for they are bread for us: their defence is departed from them, and the LORD is with us: fear them not" (Num. 14:7-9). What made Joshua and Caleb different from the other 10 spies? How could they so confidently assert, "Fear them not"?

I believe the key can be found in Luke 14:31-32: "Or what king, going to make war against another king, sitteth not down first, and consulteth whether he be able with ten thousand to meet him that cometh against him with twenty thousand? Or else, while the other is yet a great way off, he sendeth an ambassage [envoy], and desireth conditions of peace." In other words, without Christ and His power, you will make peace with your enemies and allow them to stay in the place that is rightfully yours.

If you are a child of God, every promise in the Word is yours, including victory over fear. However, you must be willing to ask yourself, *Do I have the power to come against an enemy that is much stronger than I am?* And you must come to the conclusion that you do not have the ability in your own strength.

Jesus continued in Luke 14:33, "So likewise, whosoever he be of you that forsaketh not all that he hath, he cannot be my disciple." He was essentially saying, "If you do not forsake all that you have—all your own efforts, strength, plans—then you cannot follow Me where I am going." You cannot, because it is a spiritual kingdom with spiritual battles. It requires a strength that is deeper and more powerful than anything you will ever have on your own.

Joshua and Caleb understood this truth. It was not pride that caused them to believe they were able to defeat the giants in the land. Rather, it was humility—knowing that victory would come only by total dependence on God. The sooner you and I get to this point of knowing that we are nothing in ourselves, the better off we will be. We are nothing in ourselves, but everything to the heart of God.

AGREE WITH YOUR ADVERSARY

The Lord appointed Joshua to lead the next generation of Israelites into the Promised Land, leaving those who were full of fear and unbelief to die in the wilderness. God's word to Joshua was, "Don't let fear or dismay get a hold of you, because it is not about you." He gives us the same reminder today that we do not have to fear, for it is not about us, it is about Christ in us.

Knowing that Joshua had to be absolutely convinced of this, the Lord allowed an encounter before they crossed over. "And it came to pass, when Joshua was by

Jericho, that he lifted up his eyes and looked, and, be-hold, there stood a man over against him with his sword drawn in his hand: and Joshua went unto him, and said unto him, Art thou for us, or for our adversaries?" (Josh. 5:13). Almost every scholar agrees that this is a pre-incarnate appearance of Jesus Christ. But He came as a man with a sword drawn in His hand, leaving Joshua un-able to determine if He was for them or against them. His sword was drawn, but His countenance said, "This far and no farther."

Jesus said it this way: "Agree with thine adversary quickly, while thou are in the way with him; lest at any time the adversary deliver thee to the judge, and the judge deliver thee to the officer, and thou be cast into prison" (Matt. 5:25). At certain times in your walk with God, He will become your adversary—not for evil, but for good. He knows that flesh cannot occupy the land of promise; it will ultimately shrink back in fear. So the Lord comes and stands before you, telling you that this is where you stop. This is where you stop relying on yourself; this is where you drop your plans about how you are going to survive the coming difficulties. You will not win this battle in your own strength. Jesus said you must agree with your adversary when you are in that sit-uation—especially if your adversary is God.

And he said, Nay; but as captain of the host of the LORD am I now come. And Joshua fell on his face to the earth, and did worship, and said unto him, What saith my Lord unto his servant? And the captain of the LORD's host said unto Joshua, Loose thy shoe from off thy foot; for the place whereon thou standest is holy. And Joshua did so (Josh. 5:14-15).

Jesus stood before Joshua, saying, "Loose your shoe from off your foot." In other words, "Not by might, nor by power, but by my spirit, saith the LORD of hosts" (Zech. 4:6). God was telling him, "I don't need your power, and I don't want your best effort or your strategies. Take off your sandals, for you are standing on holy ground. It is a sacred place where God alone will bring you through, and God alone will be glorified!" It is a lesson the Lord began to teach me even as a young Christian.

I had been set free from panic attacks for a few years when one day I was approached by a member of the police department I was working for and asked to become a public figure. It was a position that would involve representing them and addressing large groups of people, so he asked me plainly if I was afraid of public speaking. "No," I confidently asserted, after which I immediately thought to myself, *What in the world am I saying?* (Bear in mind that at this point, the prospect of speaking before crowds of people was still terrifying.)

As part of the training, they sent me to an instructional school for public speaking. I found myself among seasoned police officers from across the country who were essentially there to refine their skills. I was the only novice in the room.

The class required each of us to do four oral presentations, beginning with a three-minute speech and culminating in a 30-minute presentation. After class, while the others would enjoy their free evenings socializing, I would be on my face, crying, "Oh, Jesus, You have to help me!"

My classmates ended up speaking on investigation techniques and other topics that were far beyond my scope of practice and experience at the time. I knew I would be no match to engage in these types of discussions, so I chose to speak on what I knew—biblical topics! For the first three speeches, I simply opened my mouth and the Holy Spirit would come, enabling me to speak freely. It was a river of life flowing that I knew was not my own.

After that point, the instructor reminded me that this was not an evangelistic association—we were being trained to represent the police department. He sternly told me that I was required to speak on a police-related topic for the 30-minute final presentation. Back to my room I went, face down, once again crying, "God, help me! I know there is no way I can do this on my own. I only ask that You be glorified!"

When the day came for giving my final presentation, I got up and said, "Today I am going to speak on a police-related topic . . . the Bible! When you and I stand in a court of law, we lay our hand on the Bible and swear to speak truthfully, based on our belief and knowledge of the contents of this book. Don't you believe it's important that we actually know what is in it?" Heads nodded, and I proceeded to speak for 30 minutes, beginning in Genesis with the fall of man and concluding in Revelation with Jesus returning as King of kings and Lord of lords!

Afterward, a panel was convened to critique me on verbal and nonverbal aspects of my public speaking—voice intonation, gestures, use of word whiskers, and so forth. Yet when they began to give their feedback, not one person mentioned any of these delivery elements. Instead, they all focused on the content of my speech. One investigator exclaimed, "Boy, have you ever given me something to think about!" Another commented,

"I have never heard anything like this in my entire life." When the course was finished, the instructor even approached me and asked if I would be willing to come back as an instructor if he were to write my department and get me released.

Clearly, it was not by my own strength or ability that I was able to do those four presentations; it was solely by the power of God. At the time, I had no idea that the Lord was preparing me for ministry—not only training me in public speaking, but also training me to become wholly dependent on Him!

It is only by the power of the Holy Spirit, not by our own strength or will, that we will be able to dispel fear and overcome whatever difficulties lie ahead. If we continue to focus on the opposition and our own insufficient strength, forgetting that the battle is the Lord's, Satan will be able to successfully wield his weapon of fear against us. When this happens, it takes us down a pathway far from what God intended for our lives.

FEAR NOT

4

WHEN FEAR TAKES CONTROL

And Saul said unto Samuel, I have sinned: for I have transgressed the commandment of the LORD, and thy words: because I feared the people, and obeyed their voice.

1 SAMUEL 15:24

M any years ago when we were living in Canada, my wife and I had a sheep farm with about 70 female sheep, some rams and a lot of lambs. Every day the flock would travel back and forth on a narrow path (the illustrations Jesus gave are truly visible in nature) no wider than perhaps a page in my Bible. It was a fairly large farm, so the sheep would often venture way back to a forest area to find relief from the summer heat. Sometimes they would wait too long before returning home, and as evening set in, they were no longer able to see the path. Once this happened, fear would begin to lead them.

If they didn't show up in the barn, I would usually grab a light and head out into the field to search for them. I actually found it quite humorous to watch them when they became fearful. The entire flock would huddle together, and I could literally sense the panic among them. Then, all of a sudden, one sheep would dart off to the left, and the whole group of 100 or so would follow, still in the huddle. They would run the width of the field until they ran into the fence!

Unable to go any farther, they would finally realize that the sheep that darted out did not actually know where it was going. So the entire flock would stop and huddle again until suddenly another sheep would bravely dart out. It was almost like those stray thoughts in our minds that, in moments of fear, cry out, "This is the way!" So the whole flock would head out, only to hit the fence again. This would continue until they utterly exhausted themselves. Finally, they would lie down on the grass and just try to pretend they were invisible. By the time I showed up, they would be so full of fear that it would take them a while to realize this was the man who would lead them to safety.

When we find ourselves in a difficult place, we are often tempted to dart out after any thought that springs up. We begin to allow the fear rising in our heart to lead us, which typically means we will end up hitting a wall. This is why it is critical not only to recognize fear as a powerful weapon used by Satan, but also to disarm him before we allow that fear to lead us astray.

Consider once again the example that God gives us through the children of Israel. They had been marvelously delivered from many years of bondage under a sinful taskmaster, as is the case with many of us today who have been delivered from lives marked with all types of bondage. God brought them out from Egypt with miraculous signs and wonders, proving that the most powerful army in the entire world could not keep captive what God said He was calling to Himself. It is a good lesson for you and me to begin to grasp—that if Christ has called us, Christ is going to keep us. If we are true children of God, we are not going to falter or fail, Satan is not going to conquer us, and our old enemies are not going to overtake us.

In spite of the fact that the children of Israel were being delivered out of Egypt, they soon realized that their enemies were marching after them. Furthermore, what lay ahead of them was literally a sea of impossibility. Fear that had not been dealt with emerged to the forefront of their hearts and led them to wrong reasoning: "And they said unto Moses, Because there were no graves in Egypt, hast thou taken us away to die in the wilderness? Wherefore hast thou dealt thus with us, to carry us forth out of Egypt? Is this not the word that we did tell thee in Egypt?" (Exod. 14:11-12).

Isn't that amazing? Moses had brought a word to the people—the very word of God. But all of a sudden, when fear rose in their hearts, they said to Moses, "We had a word for you too! You should have listened to us. We told you that we were all going to die out here, and we were right!" Of course, this was the voice of wrong reasoning. Fear will always try to come back to your heart and say, "I told you so! I told you that if you abandoned yourself to God, the pathway would be disastrous!"

Unfortunately, wrong reasoning leads to wrong conclusions. The people told Moses, "It had been better for us to serve the Egyptians, than that we should die in the wilderness" (Exod. 14:12). It would have been better! I shouldn't have left my old job. I shouldn't have followed this leading. I shouldn't have stayed in this marriage. I shouldn't have stayed in this city. All along I had this inner instinct (as many people call it, although it is simply another name for fear)—another voice that was saying, "No! If you stay here you are going to starve. You will end up worse off than if you had just gone your own way."

A STRANGE MIXTURE OF FEAR AND FAITH

Wrong reasoning leads to a wrong conclusion, which eventually results in a wrong action. People who embrace wrong reasoning ultimately end up building another pathway for themselves and forming some other image of God.

We see a clear picture of this in the life of Saul—the man God had anointed to be king. Saul was called to lead the Israelites into victory, and he was given a very definitive word from God through Samuel: "And thou shalt go down before me to Gilgal; and, behold, I will come down unto thee, to offer burnt offerings, and to sacrifice sacrifices of peace offerings: seven days shalt thou tarry, till I come to thee, and show thee what thou shalt do" (1 Sam. 10:8).

Saul did not wait for the appointed time. He went ahead and offered the burnt offering. When Samuel arrived and asked what he had done, Saul explained:

> Because I saw that the people were scattered from me [now, this is fear], and that thou camest not within the days appointed, and that the Philistines gathered themselves together at Michmash; therefore said I, The Philistines will come down now upon me to Gilgal, and I have not made supplication unto the LORD: I forced myself therefore, and offered a burnt offering. And Samuel said to Saul, Thou hast done foolishly: thou hast not kept the commandment of the LORD thy God, which he commanded thee: for now would the LORD have established thy kingdom upon Israel forever (1 Sam. 13:11-13).

When I read these words, I cannot help but wonder how many people throughout the history of the Christian church have followed the same course of action as Saul. Because God seemingly does not show up when they think He should, they take over the reins and begin to follow their own leading.

That is exactly what Saul did. He allowed fear to grip his heart, even though he was given a clear and distinct word from God. Saul essentially explained to Samuel, "Well, basically my back was to the wall, and God did not show up, so somebody had to do something." Saul presented it almost as if it was an excuse, but in reality, it was a veiled accusation against God. Saul had become his own priest, and he began to take over, directing and leading his own life. Yet it was not faith that was leading him—it was fear.

You and I would be wise to learn the lesson that Saul missed. Trust is not something that develops in us when things are going well. We have to learn to trust God when things do not look like they are going well—when we come to a place of impossibility and fear begins to overcome us. That is exactly where I found myself when I was in Burundi.

In 2007, the president of Burundi invited me to come and plead for reconciliation between the Hutus, Tutsis and Twa people. At the time, Burundi was still in an unstable state—enmity lingered among the nation's ethnic groups after the recent civil war where approximately 300,000 people were killed. When one tribe took over, they often would literally annihilate the others, so I knew that if there were to be another outbreak, there would undoubtedly be casualties among us.

Suddenly, the enemy began to plant fear in my mind about having brought a team of about 200 with me from our church in New York. I remember waking up the first couple of nights, literally hearing screams and explosions. During those moments, I had to learn to trust God, despite the fact that in the natural it was so easy to become overwhelmed by fear. I constantly had to pray and rehearse what God had spoken to me and what He promised to do.

In the end, God certainly did all that He had promised. The open-air crusade was heard over the radio waves throughout Burundi, even extending as far as Tanzania, the Congo and Rwanda. Ironically, I was speaking over the same airwaves that had been used in Rwanda to incite the genocide.

The pastors' conference turned out to be one of the most momentous times in my life. I reminded the group that if the nation was to be reconciled, it had to begin with the spiritual leaders being reconciled one to another—meaning that they had to choose to extend forgiveness to those who had harmed them. I was well aware that this was not a light request, as many of them had family members who had been murdered.

Suddenly, someone began to cry—a cry deeper than I had ever heard in my life. It started spreading, eventually turning into a corporate wail. Then, all of a sudden, incredible joy broke out among the people, and they began singing and dancing! That evening, even the vice president himself danced! We had witnessed a miracle. The president and his cabinet heeded the message that God had given them, and they did what was in their power to promote reconciliation and allow equal access to economic empowerment among all the tribes. And, of course, the entire team and I returned to New York safely.

God has promised that He will never fail us nor forsake us, but we must learn to wait upon Him in faith and obey His voice, despite what fears may begin to arise in our hearts. In Burundi, I knew that I had to believe and follow all that God had instructed me to do—even on those nights when I was tempted to succumb to intense fear.

Unfortunately, we see further on in 1 Samuel that Saul had obviously not learned his lesson, for once again he began obeying other voices due to fear. The Lord had given him another set of clear instructions: "Now go and smite Amalek, and utterly destroy all that they have, and spare them not; but slay both man and woman, infant and suckling, ox and sheep, camel and ass" (1 Sam. 15:3).

Saul and the Israelites did destroy the Amalekites, but they ended up sparing King Agag and the best of the livestock. When confronted, Saul insisted twice that he had obeyed the voice of the Lord before finally acknowledging, "I have sinned: for I have transgressed the commandment of the LORD, and thy words: because I feared the people, and obeyed their voice" (1 Sam. 15:24).

That is exactly what fear does. It gives entrance to voices other than the voice of God, and we begin to allow ourselves to be led by them. The end result is a strange mixture of fear and faith. Saul had a clear word from the Lord, but he seemingly could not obey it because fear and faith had become equal partners in his walk with God.

Within the Christian church, there are many people who give fear and faith almost equal access to operate in their lives. On Sunday they believe; on Monday they are full of fear; on Tuesday they are back to faith; on Wednesday they are full of fear again. They hear what God is saying, but at the same time their ears are attuned to what other voices are saying. Many people cannot stand because of this divided heart, and they are left unable to finish the journey in victory. As Jesus Himself said, "Every kingdom divided against itself is brought to desolation; and a house divided against a house [itself] falls" (Luke 11:17).

A heart of faith never lets fear determine action. I am not saying that as Christians we do not go through periods where our hearts become afraid. However, we must never let fear begin to lead us. God has given us very clear instructions and promises, and we must allow faith to lead us. At some point in our walk with the Lord, His words must take precedence over the fears that arise in our hearts. We must start believing God so that He will be able to show Himself faithful.

STAND STILL AND SEE

Today you may realize that fear has caused you to embrace a measure of wrong reasoning. This, in turn, has led you to wrong conclusions about the faithfulness of God—about where He is leading you and how He is going to get you there. It is important for you to address these wrong conclusions before they lead you to wrong actions, for wrong actions can easily develop into a life pattern.

How does the Lord stop this whole progression of wrong reasoning, wrong conclusions and wrong actions in our lives? I believe God sends His Word, and it is actually a very simple word. Sometimes that is all we are going to get, and it is just a matter of our believing it: "And Moses said unto the people, Fear ye not, stand still, and see the salvation of the LORD" (Exod. 14:13). Moses was warning the people not to let fear lead and govern them—not to let it mold their thinking or distort their image of God. Instead, they were to stand still and see the salvation of the Lord!

It is amazing when you look at these words in the original text. The word "see" is *ra'ah*, and it means "to see intellectually; to view something; to hear; to experience; to enjoy; or to have a position of trust." Many people get into trouble because they make decisions before they know what God is speaking. They cannot hear Him saying, "Stop! Stop talking; get off the phone; stop asking for opinions. Just come back to Me and stand still! I will cause you to see something, to hear something, to experience something that will settle you in a position of trust. Stand still and see My salvation!"

God has often had to remind me of this. With things coming at me from every side, decisions that had to be made, mini-catastrophes evolving, voices emerging from around every corner and down every corridor, the Lord has had to speak to my heart and say, "Stop! Just stop and open the Bible; sit down and read it. Stand still and one more time see My salvation. Don't make any decisions when you don't know what to do."

Interestingly, the word "salvation" in the original Hebrew text is *Yeshua*. Stand still and see *Yeshua*! *Yeshua* means "deliverance for your distress which comes from outside of your situation." God says, "I have a deliverer for you, and the deliverer has a name—*Yeshua*. Stand still and see *Yeshua*!" Stand still and come to an understanding of who God has provided for you. See the victory of God; see the triumphing power of God in *Yeshua*. See it and learn to trust Him!

A GREAT DIVIDING

After Moses exhorted the people to stand still and see God's salvation, he "stretched out his hand over the sea; and the LORD caused the sea to go back by a strong east wind all that night, and made the sea dry land, and the waters were divided" (Exod. 14:21). Remember that God also spoke in the beginning and divided the waters above from the waters beneath (see Gen. 1:6-7). In other words, one of the things that God will do when you simply stop and get back into His Word is separate the reasoning that comes from above from that which is from beneath. There is a heavenly wisdom and there is an earthly reasoning. There is the wisdom of truth and victory, and there is the human reasoning of fear and failure.

The moment we stop and return to God's Word, a great dividing takes place. We begin to look in the Bible and say, "Aha! That is what I was thinking, but *this* is what God is saying. Now I see that fear was causing me to succumb to false reasoning, which was leading me to embrace false conclusions, steering me toward a course of wrong action. But now I hear God telling me, 'Fear not, stand still and see the salvation of the Lord one more time.'"

The children of Israel went into the midst of the Red Sea on dry ground, and the waters became a wall to them on both sides. Could it be that when the Israelites went through this impossible place and the waters were gathered up, it was symbolic of a wall of protection? As we remain in His Word, God promises to take us from the point where we are now through to the other side. He promises that His Word is going to be a wall to us on the right and on the left. He promises that no power of hell can follow us through our journey with Him.

However, we must refuse to give fearful thoughts a lodging place in our hearts and reject the distorted image of God that the enemy wants to plant in our minds. As we stand still in the Word of God, the Lord will be faithful to dispel our fears and drown all the enemies pursuing us. You and I will see that it is indeed possible to walk this journey led by faith rather than by fear.

FEAR NOT

5

WHEN FAILURE GIVES WAY TO FEAR

*After these things the word of the L*ORD *came unto
Abram in a vision, saying, Fear not, Abram: I am thy shield,
and thy exceeding great reward.*

GENESIS 15:1

In this encounter between the Lord and Abraham, we have the first recorded use of the words "fear not" in the Bible. It is significant that the Lord spoke those words "after these things." To what things does this verse refer?

To find our answer, let's take a look at what occurred in Abraham's life prior to this point, starting at the beginning of his journey. I believe you will discover another realm of freedom within the words "fear not."

> Now the LORD had said unto Abram, Get thee out of thy country, and from thy kindred, and from thy father's house, unto a land that I will shew thee: and I will make of thee a great nation, and I will bless thee, and make thy name great; and thou shalt be a blessing: and I will bless them that bless thee, and curse him that curseth thee: and in thee shall all families of the earth be blessed (Gen. 12:1-3).

What an incredible command! God was calling Abraham to leave his people, his land and all that he was familiar with in order to journey to a place that was unknown to him. Accompanying this command was the incredible promise that God would bless him and bless many people through him. Can you imagine God appearing to you today and saying something similar? Actually, He already has—in Christ. He has called you out of this fallen world and into His kingdom of light, and now the same promises that were given to Abraham are yours in Christ.

In obedience and faith, Abraham headed out with his wife and his nephew toward the Promised Land. In the same way, you and I began this journey with incredible promises set before us. We knew from the Scriptures that God promised us a new mind, a new heart, a new spirit and new direction. We were confident we would become the people that God destined us to be in the earth, however that should unfold in each of our lives.

However, Abraham was not long into his journey when that deadly enemy fear confronted him. He had made it to Canaan and was within the physical borders of what God had promised him. Yet in that land of promise, a severe famine had set in. Most likely out of fear for his own provision, Abraham left and went down to Egypt—only to now be confronted with the fear of losing his life on account of his beautiful wife.

The common practice of a king of these foreign nations when he saw a beautiful woman was to take her into his own harem. If she happened to be married, no problem—he would simply kill her husband, and suddenly she would be available for marriage again. Abraham was well aware of this practice as he and Sarah entered Egypt. Fearing for his life, he came up with a plan. "Listen, Sarai, just tell them that you are my sister. Then they will not kill me, and you will be safe as well" (see Gen. 12:11-13). Abraham had given into fear. And so we have a picture of what tends to be the bottom line of most of our fears: fear for our safety. We fear not having enough to eat; we fear not being able to pay the rent. At the root of it all is the fear that we are going to die.

Abraham and his wife eventually left Egypt, and soon both Abraham and his nephew, Lot, began to experience an increase of their livestock to the point that the land could no longer handle their living in such close proximity. Disputes began to break out between their herdsmen, and subsequently, Abraham had to endure a separation from members of his own family (see Gen. 13:5-12). Perhaps you have had a similar experience. In the time that you have known Christ, you have found that family members, or those who were once like family to you, have rejected you and gone their own way—which may in turn give rise to a fear that you have somehow failed in these relationships.

Later, Abraham had to fight in a small-scale war when his nephew was taken into captivity by foreign kings who plundered Sodom and Gomorrah. Abraham armed his household, a few hundred men, and went in pursuit of the captors (see Gen. 14:11-14). We, too, are often drawn into battles over family members who have been brought into captivity by the enemy. How easy it is at that point to become disheartened over their failures—to fear that the promises God has spoken regarding our family will not hold true in their lives.

And so Genesis 15 tells us that after all these things, God came to Abraham and said, "Fear not, I am your protection, and I am the One who is your reward." In other words, "Despite all these things that have happened, what I told you I was going to do, I am going to do. My promise still stands!"

PUTTING THE PROMISE IN JEOPARDY

Although he eventually went on to become known as the "father of faith," we have seen that Abraham was certainly not a man without faults. I am thankful that the Scriptures have recorded these things, for it gives hope to you and me today, reminding us that none are exempt from giving in to fear from time to time. And even more important, it allows us to get a glimpse of God's character and His mercy in light of our faltering steps and failures.

Notice that when Abraham told Sarah to lie about their relationship and pretend to be only his sister, he was indirectly taking the promise of God and putting it into a place where it could not be fulfilled. That is what fear does! Abraham had been given the promise of a son, and through that son would come a lineage as numerous as the stars of the heaven. These would be the patriarchs of Israel, leading straight to Jesus Christ and to His church. Of course, in order for the promise to be fulfilled, this seed had to go through his wife, Sarah. Yet, in a moment of fear, Abraham put his wife into a place where the promise could no longer be fulfilled—in the harem of another man's house.

I can picture Abraham standing outside the gate of Pharaoh's court lamenting, "Oh, God, through my fear I lost the promise!" That is precisely the time when the devil will find an opportunity to slip in with one of his last ploys: "Well, you had a promise, but you lost it. You gave it up, and now somebody else has it captive. You can never get it back."

At that time, Pharaoh happened to be the most powerful military ruler on the earth. There were probably hundreds, if not thousands, of soldiers guarding Pharaoh's harem. There was literally no way that Abraham could get

Sarah back; and without Sarah, there would be no fulfillment of the promise. All the while, the devil would be right there with his incessant taunting: "Abraham, just get lost and go home. Go back to Ur of the Chaldeans. Give it all up! You have already lost the promise because of fear anyway."

Of course, that is not how the story ends. "And the LORD plagued Pharaoh and his house with great plagues because of Sarai Abram's wife" (Gen. 12:17).

Imagine the astonishment in Pharaoh's house when everybody suddenly broke out in a loathsome disease! "And Pharaoh called Abram, and said, What is this that thou hast done unto me? Why didst thou not tell me that she was thy wife? Why saidst thou, She is my sister? So I might have taken her to me to wife: now therefore behold thy wife, take her, and go thy way" (Gen. 12:18-19). Not only that, but also Pharaoh even sent Abraham away with all the sheep, oxen, menservants and maidservants he had given him!

The plan of God for Abraham's life had not been aborted—his wife was divinely returned in spite of the fact that Abraham had given in to fear. Suddenly the gate of what looked like hell opened wide, and out came Sarah and the promise, just as beautiful as it had always been. What joy must have flooded Abraham's heart! Imagine how he must have leapt and danced as not only Sarah came out of the gate, but also an abundance of livestock and provision for the journey.

Little did Abraham know, but he was about to have a visitation from the Lord Himself. Christ was going to come to his tent and say, "Now it is time for the promise to be fulfilled. This time next year you are going to have a son, and his name is going to be 'laughter' because you are going to be so filled with the joy of the Lord that all you can do is laugh" (see Gen. 18:9-10; 21:6).

HIS PROMISE STILL STANDS

Perhaps your great fear today is that you have failed God, and now you think you have been relegated to a lesser plan for your life. Yet no matter what your failures, no matter how you may have allowed the voice of fear to lead you to places where the fulfillment of God's promise seems impossible, take heart! After all of these things, God has a word for you today: "Fear not!" His promise still stands.

We must often remind ourselves of this assurance, particularly in the midst of our failures. God cannot lie; every promise in the Bible is yours as a believer in Christ. That is why you must read the Word and meditate on it until it becomes your mind; until you begin to realize who you are in Christ Jesus. God is your shield from all the lies the devil will throw at you—lies that you are not who God says you are, that you are not going to achieve what God says you will. The Lord would remind you, "Not only am I your shield, but I am also the One who spoke those things into your life, and what I said, I am going to do." That has always been the miracle of the gospel, the wonderment of being part of the church of Jesus Christ. God help us when we try to figure out how to do for ourselves, through our own wisdom and strategies, what God is determined to do for us.

Yes, there may be times when we momentarily give in to fear; but deep down, we know whom we have believed, and we are persuaded that He is able to keep that which we have committed to Him (see 2 Tim. 1:12). We may fall, but every time we do, the Lord will raise us up again—just as He did Abraham.

Therefore, don't forget that in spite of your failings, the plan of God is as real in your life today as it was on the day He first whispered it to you. He is going to bring "Sarah" back to you; He is going to make His promise alive in your heart once again, and you are going to glorify Him in this generation. So fear not—even your greatest failures do not have the power to nullify the Word of God!

FEAR NOT

6

GOD HAS NOT GIVEN US A SPIRIT OF FEAR

*For God hath not given us the spirit of fear; but of power,
and of love, and of a sound mind.*

2 TIMOTHY 1:7

Sometimes all you need is one stone. When I was a young Christian, this verse in 2 Timothy was the only stone I had against the giant of fear. Yet over and over it helped me move forward during those moments when I was tempted to stay paralyzed by fear. It was powerful then, and even more so now that God has deepened my understanding of the incredible truth contained within those words. As children of God, we do not have to live in fear—a spirit that does not come from Him. Instead, we have the liberty to choose to walk in what the Lord *does* offer us.

A SPIRIT OF POWER

It is amazing to me how many people want the power of Christ but not the path of Christ. They do not want to follow a Christ who uses His resources and power to help others. However, they will soon discover that following Jesus inevitably leads to a road of self-sacrifice. It is at this crossroads that many turn away from following the Jesus of the Bible.

We see in the Scriptures that multitudes came to Jesus because they were hungry and saw that He could multiply bread. Others came because they wanted to rule and reign, and they thought Jesus would overthrow the Roman Empire. What Jesus was asking for, however, was full commitment to the cause of God that was about to be unfolded in His life. He told them, "It is the spirit that quickeneth; the flesh profiteth nothing: the words that I speak unto you, they are spirit, and they are life" (John 6:63). In other words, "What I am telling you will give you life, carry you, sustain you and keep you through difficult days." Jesus added, "But there are some of you that believe not," for He "knew from the beginning who they were that believed not, and who should betray him" (v. 64).

When they recognized what it would cost, many disciples turned away and walked with Him no more. I believe this is how it will play out in our day too. When the truth of Christ is proclaimed, many people will realize that they did not sign up to be a representation of God's life in the midst of a hostile generation. Suddenly it is no longer very attractive—God is asking for a commitment that will take them to a cross.

Scripture does not say the people abandoned religion; rather, they abandoned Jesus Christ. In other words, they returned to "a form of godliness, but denying the power thereof" (2 Tim. 3:5). They went back to a form of religion, and perhaps they were even more zealous than before. But all of it was powerless. They went back to powerless singing, powerless reading and powerless praying—all because they were confronted with what a life of following Christ is truly supposed to look like.

I believe that in these last days there will be a rise of religion everywhere—a feel-good religion that will become the religion of the day. "I'm okay, you're okay! We're all in this together, and everything is going to be alright!" In reality, they will close the door of their hearts to where the real life and power of God is. They will have a form of godliness that is actually a denial of what the gospel is all about: *the power of God that transforms people.*

On the other hand, the apostle Paul was someone who clearly was willing to follow the path of Christ no matter what the cost. When he and his companions were in Caesarea, a prophet named Agabus bound his own feet and hands with Paul's belt and said, "Thus saith the Holy Ghost, So shall the Jews at Jerusalem bind the man that owneth this girdle, and shall deliver him into the hands of the Gentiles" (Acts 21:11). When those around Paul saw and heard this prophecy, they tried to convince him not to go to Jerusalem. But Paul answered, "I am ready not to be bound only, but also to die at Jerusalem for the name of the Lord Jesus" (Acts 21:13). He would not be persuaded otherwise, so finally those with him said, "The will of the Lord be done" (v. 14).

Later, the Lord stood by Paul and said, "Be of good cheer, Paul; for as you have testified for Me in Jerusalem, so you must also bear witness at Rome" (Acts 23:11, *NJKV*). And when Paul was in the midst of a tremendous storm and the entire ship was falling apart—as much of our present society is starting to do—God said, "Fear not, Paul; thou must be brought before Caesar" (Acts 27:24). God was telling him, "You are going to go in chains before this ruler and before those who think they are in authority, when in reality they are not. You will be given as a witness to testify before them." Obviously it was not the most appealing assignment, but that was the will of God for Paul's life.

Because Paul willingly embraced God's will, he received a spirit of power and was able to stand up in the midst of the storm and exhort the rest of the fearful crew, "Be of good cheer: for there shall be no loss of any man's life among you, but of the ship. For there stood by me this night the angel of God, whose I am, and whom I serve, saying, Fear not, Paul . . . God hath given thee all them that sail with thee. Wherefore, sirs, be of good cheer: for I believe God, that it shall be even as it was told me" (Acts 27:22-25). The Lord had given Paul the 276 people on the ship with him because he embraced the will of God rather than fearing for his own life in the storm.

Jesus explained it to His disciples this way: "My meat is to do the will of him that sent me, and to finish his work" (John 4:34). In other words, "I have a source of strength that you are not aware of yet. My strength is found in doing the will of God. This is what feeds my life; it is what empowers me to get up in the morning and not be overwhelmed with what I have to face that day. It gives me power to endure the scorn, the rejection, the voices opposing me."

Jesus continued, "Say not ye, There are yet four months, and then cometh harvest? Behold, I say unto you, lift up your eyes, and look on the fields; for they are white already to harvest. And he that reapeth receiveth wages, and gathereth fruit unto life eternal: that both he that soweth and he that reapeth may rejoice together" (John 4:35-36). How often do we say that revival is near, that the harvest is coming? According to Jesus it is already here, ready to be harvested! The wages are provision, meaning that if you go into the harvest to do the work of God, you will receive an infusion of power and strength. God will indwell you as His physical temple on the earth, empowering you to continue His work of bringing mankind to redemption.

God desires to give each of us this spirit of power—power to be other than who we are. He would never call us to be something He did not enable us to be. However, you and I will never know the full power of God until we are living for the purposes of God in the earth. There is no true power found in anything else.

We may read many books and attend seminars on how to live a powerful life, but the true power of God is ultimately found in reaching the lost. Once we are determined to give ourselves for the purposes of God and for the people around us, this Spirit of power will be realized in our lives. The Spirit will give us a word for those around us; we will stand in the storm, and lives will be spared.

A SPIRIT OF LOVE

Not only will we be given a spirit of power, but we will also be given a spirit of love. Love is the work of God. "For God so loved the world, that he gave his only begotten Son" (John 3:16). There is a genuine love of God that flows from the heart of those who are given to His work. Paul was able to stand up and exhort those on the ship with him, for he was given a love for the very people who refused to listen to his warnings not to set sail in the first place.

Later, as Paul approached the end of his life, he wrote to Timothy, "Be not thou therefore ashamed of the testimony of our Lord, nor of me his prisoner: but be thou partaker of the afflictions of the gospel according to the power of God" (2 Tim. 1:8). The word "ashamed" here does not mean to blush and hide in the corner—it means to be overpowered, to be triumphed over. In other words, don't be overpowered by what might lie before you. Don't be triumphed over by it, and don't be turned back from it.

Paul was writing to Timothy from jail, and he knew that the end of his course was coming soon. Some of his final instructions to Timothy were, "Don't be turned back by these afflictions. Don't live your life trying to find a safe haven for yourself because that will only culminate in fear. Rather, give yourself to the work of God. Be a partaker of whatever you have to go through for the sake of other people and for the glory of God."

It was Paul who penned the words, "Love is not self-seeking" (1 Cor. 13:5). He understood this truth about love. He was aware that the outcome of a life not seeking its own but instead lived for others would result in freedom from fear, for "there is no fear in love" (1 John 4:18). By contrast, along with selfishness inevitably comes fear. Recall the evening when Jesus set sail with His disciples after giving them the word that they were going to cross to the other side. Suddenly a storm hit and the boat began to fill with water, sending the disciples into a panic. When they found Jesus asleep at the back of the boat, they awakened Him and began to accuse Him, "Master, carest thou not that we perish?" (Mark 4:38).

The disciples were so full of fear for their own lives that they neglected the fact that there were also other little boats traveling with them—yet they were the ones who actually had Jesus in their boat! Likewise, whatever storm we may find ourselves in, we must realize that there are many others in the same storm. However, we are the ones who have the Savior in our life, in our very own boat, meaning that there is no way we are going down. We have been given the Word of God that says we are going to make it to the other side. Therefore, we do not have to worry about saving ourselves; instead, we are free to embrace the work of God in saving the lost. As we take our eyes off of ourselves and enter into the work of God, we will be empowered by a spirit of love rather than driven by a spirit of fear.

Consider the words of Jesus as He alluded to His death days before His crucifixion: "Now is my soul troubled; and what shall I say? Father, save me from this hour: but for this cause came I unto this hour. Father, glorify thy name" (John 12:27-28). Many times we find ourselves in the midst of a storm or trial, and our continual cry to the Lord is, "Save me!" Yet the Son of God, facing death on a cross, did not draw back in fear nor try to save His life. Instead, a spirit of love sent Him willingly to the cross to lay down His life for all humanity. In the same way, many people's lives will be spared as you make the choice to embrace the will of God, moving you away from fear and bringing you into the work of God, empowered by His love.

A SOUND MIND

In the near future, many things that appear in the news are going to cause fear. It is during such unsettled times that many voices will try to surface in your mind. Some will be your own fears seeking to dominate your thoughts; others will be false reasoning sent by the devil himself. All these voices will be working to destroy your ability to stand strong in difficult days. Unfortunately, there will be multitudes of people who will become prey to anyone and everyone claiming to speak for God. Because they were never truly surrendered to the Word of God or His will for their lives, they will be given over to their own way—to a reprobate mind rather than a sound mind (see Rom. 1:28).

In this hour, when a myriad of voices and false prophets are emerging, we must recognize how imperative it is to have a sound mind, clearly discerning God's voice and allowing ourselves to be directed by truth. If you choose to turn to God with all your heart, He will begin revealing His Word and His voice to you. "And thine ears shall hear a word behind thee, saying, This is the way, walk ye in it, when ye turn to the right hand, and when ye turn to the left" (Isa. 30:21).

God will give you a sound mind if that is your desire. He will take you into the Scriptures and you will be established in the ways of God, able to discern truth. Soon you will get to the point where you are no longer fighting in your mind, no longer governed by your own natural thinking. That means you will not be moved by what other people are saying or by what you see in the news. You will not be overcome with fear at every evil report you hear, for you will know what is right and what the Bible says. You will remember what God has spoken to you, and as you walk in what He says, you will live to see it fulfilled. All hell can send its deepest, darkest enemies against you, but you will have the confidence that one line of truth can send the whole crew to flight. "If God be for us, who can be against us?" (Rom. 8:31). Or when fears about provision for the future arise, suddenly you will remember David's words: "I have been young, and now am old; yet I have not seen the righteous forsaken, nor his descendants begging bread" (Ps. 37:25, *NKJV*).

The major difference between people with a sound mind and those without will be evidenced by God's leading in their lives. David wrote, "He maketh me to lie down in green pastures: he leadeth me beside the still waters" (Ps. 23:2). Those with a sound mind will be led by the tender voice of their Savior, and they will be given promises of reassurance no matter what they face in the coming days. God will grant them quietness in their souls and confidence in the midst of conflict and fear. They will have the ability to hear God tell them, "I have already prepared a table for you. You must go through strong battles ahead, but along the way there is an incredible banquet of truth, and you will be able to stop and partake of the finest food available. You will be sustained and strengthened all the way along this journey. You will come to the awareness that it is not your old fears, but rather the goodness and mercy of God following you and triumphing over every enemy."

If you will choose to embrace the will of God for your life, you will be astounded at what He will make available for you. Power, love and a sound mind—that is what comes from God, and it comes only from God.

Trust Him for the power to be all that He has called you to be. Determine in your heart to find His will and enter His work, and God will do His part to fill you with the Holy Spirit who will overpower any spirit of fear.

FEAR NOT

7

HE WILL GIVE HIS ANGELS CHARGE OVER YOU

There shall no evil befall thee, neither shall any plague come nigh thy dwelling. For he shall give his angels charge over thee, to keep thee in all thy ways. They shall bear thee up in their hands, lest thou dash thy foot against a stone.

PSALM 91:10-12

Psalm 91 is a favorite of many Christians, particularly when praying God's protection over their lives. Understandably so, as the Lord gives many distinct promises to defend and keep His people from evil and harm. However, I wonder how many people truly walk in the freedom of these verses. Consider, for example, Psalm 91:5: "Thou shalt not be afraid for the terror by night; nor for the arrow that flieth by day."

Could it be possible that there is a way to simply quote the promises of God, yet another way to walk in the fullness and reality of those promises? I believe the answer will begin to unfold as we take a closer look at the temptations Jesus faced in the wilderness and how He ultimately lived to see God's Word fulfilled in His life. Our desire should be to walk as Jesus did—in the reality of God's promises, especially as we face a season when so many will be gripped by fear.

TEMPTATION IN THE WILDERNESS

Often the temptations we must endure occur at the time of our greatest usefulness to the kingdom of God. Suddenly we find ourselves violently opposed in our minds and hearts with thoughts trying to push us away from what God has called us to be in Christ. In light of this, bear in mind that in a season when men's hearts are failing them for fear, it is potentially the Church's finest hour to rise up for the sake of the kingdom of God. This means that you and I are likely to find ourselves in places that are very undesirable to the flesh—a type of personal wilderness. We see this all throughout the Scriptures.

We see it recorded in the Old Testament when Joseph was right at the stage where he was going to be given the keys to an incredible food supply in the midst of a famine. God was going to give him wisdom and authority to make a difference in the earth, but first Joseph had to spend many years in a prison cell in his own wilderness.

Though Moses was called of God to deliver the Israelites out of captivity, he had to spend 40 years in the wilderness prior to being used to speak to Pharaoh.

David, who was anointed to be king over Israel, once said, "I looked on my right hand, and beheld, but there was no man that would know me: refuge failed me; no man cared for my soul" (Ps. 142:4). He was in a cave with nothing attractive about it, yet he was at the threshold of fulfilling the very purpose for his life.

Even Jesus was led into a wilderness place—a place where He would be tempted to abandon the ultimate purpose for His life: "And Jesus being full of the Holy

Ghost returned from Jordan, and was led by the Spirit into the wilderness, being forty days tempted of the devil" (Luke 4:1-2). Jesus was about three years away from fulfilling the calling that was given to Him by His Father—three years away from the greatest event ever recorded in the world, where the Son of God died for the sins of the world. He was so close to the finish line, and that is exactly when the devil came and tempted Him the hardest.

Satan knew that Jesus was on a redemptive mission, but he did not know exactly how it was going to play out, for the Scripture says, "None of the princes of this world knew: for had they known it, they would not have crucified the Lord of glory" (1 Cor. 2:8). All the devil knew was that he had stolen humanity in the Garden of Eden and that Jesus was determined to take back what was stolen. Somehow Satan would have to tempt Jesus and divert Him from this pathway that was before His life.

Just as Satan tempted Jesus in the wilderness, we are going to be temped in these last days to abandon the cross and the call of God on our lives. Everything that we have ever known is beginning to change. In this time of calamity, this wilderness, you and I are going to be tempted like we have never been tempted before. I will show you how this temptation is going to play out.

A SELF-FOCUS

We see in the Scriptures that the wilderness temptations occurred in a specific sequence. First came self-focus: "And Jesus . . . was led by the Spirit into the wilderness, being forty days tempted of the devil. And in those days he did eat nothing: and when they were ended, he afterward hungered. And the devil said unto him, If thou be the Son of God, command this stone that it be made bread" (Luke 4:1-3).

In other words, "Use your personal relationship with God for your own needs. Focus on yourself!" That was the temptation, and that will always be a temptation in the time of fear. We have witnessed it over and over whenever a calamity hits—people raiding stores, trying to secure their own food and water. The reason is because self-focus is accompanied by fear—the need to be our own security, find our own provision, fulfill our own needs.

On the other hand, freedom from fear comes from being focused on others. Jesus did not come to earth to live for Himself; He came to live solely for the will of His Father. That is why He lived His life without any bondage to fear. Jesus knew and accepted that the will of His Father was to send Him to a cross. He told His disciples, "Let these sayings sink down into your ears: for the Son of man shall be delivered into the hands of men" (Luke 9:44).

The devil came to Jesus in His moment of weakness and need and said, "Focus on Yourself. You are hungry. You have needs. Command that this stone be made into bread. Just do things a little bit differently." It is the same tactic Satan continues to use today—trying to promote the idea that serving God does not need to involve hardship. As a child of God, you have been given power— so shouldn't you use it to help yourself and escape difficult situations?

Thank God that Satan did not succeed in diverting Jesus to self-focus in the wilderness, for who knows what that would have meant for Gethsemane? If Jesus had not had this fixed determination to live for others rather than for Himself—if He had not understood that the purpose of His life was to be given for you and me— how easy it would have been to shrink back from the cross in fear.

AN ILLUSION OF VICTORY

The next tactic of the temptation was an appeal to pride: "And the devil, taking him up into an high mountain, showed unto him all the kingdoms of the world in a moment of time. And the devil said unto him, All this power will I give thee, and the glory of them: for that is delivered unto me; and to whomsoever I will I give it. If thou therefore wilt worship me, all shall be thine" (Luke 4:5-7).

The devil took Jesus to a high mountain—a place of pride—and said to Him, "You have come to rule and reign, haven't You? You have come to reclaim that which has been lost to God. If this is what You have come for, You don't need to finish the journey—I will give it to You now. All You have to do is bend Your knee to me and agree that God's way is not the only way to get things done. There are other ways to do it."

What the devil was offering Jesus was simply an illusion of victory. Satan was offering Him a throne over the kingdoms of this world, but He would be ruling over an unredeemed humanity, for redemption could only come through the cross. When we abandon the cross and all that it requires of us, refusing to take it up daily and follow Jesus as He followed His Father, we end up with an illusion of victory. That's all it is—an illusion.

I think of all the churches in our generation that have abandoned the cross of Jesus Christ. There is no cross in the theology they preach, but rather all that is spoken is for the purpose of making men feel better about themselves. There is no cross, no repentance, no turning from sin, no hunger for the Word of God. Consequently, there is very little evangelism that is based in truth. A kingdom has been built, but it is merely an illusion; it is not the church of Jesus Christ.

The Bible says that every man's work is going to be tried by fire to prove what it is made of (see 1 Cor. 3:13). We are all about to go into a fire—into seasons in this world that are almost unthinkable to the natural mind. The churches that are built on another foundation may be filled with thousands of people, but that is just an illusion with no weight or substance to it. Therefore, when the trials and difficulties come, just like the Scripture says, the people will be offended (see Matt. 24:10).

Unfortunately, many of these people will end up in fear after living so long under the false theology that the sole purpose of Jesus' coming was to make their life wonderful. They thought Jesus was going to give them a better personality, a bigger house, a promotion on their job. Yet when things take a turn and are not going as anticipated—when they lose their job, their family is in trouble, life situations are not going well, they are suffering from depression—many will be offended. None of this will fit into their theology anymore, and many will be overtaken by confusion and fear. They will not know who the real Jesus is; therefore, they will be unable to believe His promises to keep His people.

WILL GOD PROTECT YOU?

Finally, the third temptation involved a more insidious threat that questioned the veracity of God: "And he brought him to Jerusalem, and set him on a pinnacle of the temple, and said unto him, If thou be the Son of God, cast thyself down from hence: for it is written, He shall give his angels charge over thee, to keep thee: and in their hands they shall bear thee up, lest at any time thou dash thy foot against a stone" (Luke 4:9-11).

I believe that veiled in this temptation was Satan saying to the Son of God, "If You persist on this course, I am going to kill You. Do You think God is going to protect You? Will He really raise You up? If I throw You off a cliff, do You think He is going to send His angels to catch You before You hit the bottom? If You believe it, then put God to the test. Jump off the pinnacle of this temple and let's see if God's Word is true!"

"And Jesus answering said unto him, It is said, Thou shalt not tempt the Lord thy God" (Luke 4:12). By this point, I believe the devil had just crossed a line—he was talking to the Lion of Judah now. He was not just talking to Jesus the man; he was talking to Jesus the Son of God. I can see Jesus looking at the devil with those eyes of fire, saying, "You will not put God to a foolish test. I don't have to test my Father, because my Father cannot lie." And so the devil ended the temptation and departed from Him for a season.

It was after this temptation that Jesus went into the temple. He stood up, opened the book of Isaiah and began to speak words that ought to be our testimony in this generation: "The Spirit of the Lord is upon me, because he hath anointed me to preach the gospel to the poor; he hath sent me to heal the brokenhearted, to preach deliverance to the captives, and recovering of sight to the blind, to set at liberty them that are bruised" (Luke 4:18). He did not say, "The Spirit of the Lord is upon me because He has anointed me to turn stones into bread. He has anointed me to establish a kingdom on this earth that has an appearance of glory. The Spirit of the Lord is upon me because He has anointed me to do signs and wonders like jumping off a cliff, and you will see angels begin to hold me up."

No, that is not why the Spirit of God was upon Him. The people who will stand in these last days without fear will be those who have the anointing of God to preach to the poor of this world—to tell them they have a Redeemer; to tell them that there is a cross; to tell them there is a way out of everything that we are experiencing in this life and a way into eternity with God.

When Jesus finished reading the prophecy about Himself in Isaiah, Scripture tells us, "And all they in the synagogue, when they heard these things, were filled with wrath, and rose up, and thrust him out of the city, and led him unto the brow of the hill whereon their city was built, that they might cast him down headlong" (Luke 4:28-29). You can see the devil is behind it now, enraging this religious crowd. In effect, Satan is saying, "I cannot divert Him and I cannot change His focus to selfishness. I cannot get Him to bend His knee and agree that the reasoning of darkness and humanity is equal to the reasoning of God. Jesus thinks that God will protect Him—that God will lift Him up. Now throw Him off a cliff!"

This is the very temptation the devil will bring to you—that if you continue to follow the path of God, it will mean harm; it will mean a threat to your life or perhaps the lives of your children. Things are going to be too difficult if you stand up as a witness in this generation, especially when everything is beginning to move against the testimony of Jesus Christ.

Look carefully at what happened next: "But he passing through the midst of them went his way" (Luke 4:30).

Now tell me, how was that possible? Bear in mind that there is hardly a deeper wrath than when you enrage a religious crowd, offending their sensibility of who they think God is. And here were possibly hundreds of people known for their vehemence, pushing Jesus to the edge of the cliff. They had the intention of actually throwing Him off—which is exactly what Satan tried to get Jesus to do on the pinnacle of the temple. Yet suddenly the crowd must have parted! The Scripture does not say that Jesus ran away or that somebody came and helped Him. It simply says that He walked through the middle of them and just went His way. How did that happen?

THE KEY TO BANISHING FEAR

It is because it is written, "He shall give his angels charge over three, to keep thee: and in their hands they shall bear thee up, lest at any time thou dash thy foot against a stone" (Luke 4:10-11). Jesus did not fulfill the Scripture by trying to preserve His own life. Rather, as Jesus walked in obedience to the Father and refused to succumb to the temptations of the devil, His life was under the covering and keeping promises of God. Jesus was fully given to the purposes of God for His life, and God was going to see the purpose of His life through to completion.

What that means to me is that my life is not over until God says it's over! Satan could not kill the Son of God before the time God allowed it to happen—until He had fulfilled His purpose for coming to the earth. So do not believe for a second that if you choose to live for Jesus Christ in this generation, somehow it is going to prematurely end your health, your safety or your life. You are in the hands of God! The Lord knows the moment, the day, the month, the week, the year that you are going to die—it is all in His hands. Once you have finally settled this truth in your heart, fear begins to subside.

Immediately after reading the portion of Scripture from the book of Isaiah, we are told, "And he closed the book . . . and he began to say unto them, This day is this scripture fulfilled in your ears" (Luke 4:20-21). There comes a point when you have to just close the book and say, "I am not open to any lies or any other opinion on my life. I know the purpose of my life, and I know that God will keep me until I fulfill it. I am closing the book on fear!

FEAR NOT

8

CHOOSE TO
FOLLOW GOD

*Praise ye the LORD. Blessed is the man that
feareth the LORD, that delighteth greatly in his
commandments. His seed shall be mighty upon earth:
the generation of the upright shall be blessed.*

PSALM 112:1-2

Psalm 112 is one of my favorite psalms. Within these verses, the Lord assures us of the security of those who are godly.

There is a reason to walk with God, a reason to read the Bible and pray. God says that He will bless your children. Even if your sons and daughters are no longer under your roof, the promise still applies to you. Just start walking with God—start going into the prayer closet and doing what the Scripture says, and you will soon realize that God is not limited as we are. Your child could be living on the other side of the world, and God will still touch him or her when you begin to walk under the covering of the Word of God. Suddenly the thought will enter your child's heart, *I need to get right with God; I need to walk with God.* I have heard the testimonies of such things happening over and over again.

Freedom from fear is the heritage of the righteous—of those who are seeking God: "Surely he shall not be moved for ever: the righteous shall be in everlasting remembrance. He shall not be afraid of evil tidings: his heart is fixed, trusting in the LORD" (Ps. 112:6-7). Those who are right with God will not be afraid of whatever comes on the news tomorrow or happens in the world around them. When Mary Magdalene and Mary the mother of James went to the tomb after Jesus was crucified, an earthquake had just occurred, and an angel of the Lord had rolled away the stone from the entrance to the tomb. When this happened, the Bible tells us the "guards shook with fear when they saw him, and they fell into a dead faint" (Matt. 28:4, *NLT*). But notice what happened next: The two Marys heard the voice of the angel speaking to them, "Fear not ye: for I know that ye seek Jesus" (Matt. 28:5).

I believe the same thing will occur in our day. Just like the guards, many people will shake in fear as they witness great calamities on the earth, but not so with those who are seeking Jesus. The people who have chosen to follow God will be able to hear and believe as the Lord speaks to them: "Fear not ye, for I know that ye seek Jesus."

CHOOSE THIS DAY

Scripture gives us an example in the book of Joshua of one who chose to follow God, listen to His voice and live a life of victory. Joshua gave instructions to the Israelites for the capture of Jericho, led the people into the Promised Land and divided the land among the tribes. At the end of his days, Joshua looked back at those who he still had to conquer. There was still much to do and still a considerable testimony needed in the Promised Land. As he was looking at those coming up behind him, Joshua issued a challenge:

> Choose you this day whom ye will serve; whether the gods which your fathers served that were on the other side of the flood, or the gods of the Amorites, in whose land ye dwell (Josh. 24:15).

Joshua was saying, "If you refuse to serve the Lord, then choose whom you are going to serve. You can serve the gods who didn't do anything for people way back through history, or you can serve the gods in the place where you now dwell who are doing nothing for the people today." Then Joshua added, "but as for me and my house, we will serve the LORD" (v. 15).

When I was a young Christian, a friend made a sign for me that was about five feet wide by about four feet high with those very words of Joshua: "But as for me and my house, we will serve the LORD." I hung it on a tree limb by the road where my farmhouse stood. At the time I didn't know where that would lead or what it would actually entail. All I knew was that I meant it. I had made the decision to go with God—determined to serve Him with all of my heart, all the days of my life.

It was determination that brought Joshua into the supernatural, and this is why the Lord gave him a specific promise at the beginning of his journey: "Have not I commanded thee? Be strong and of a good courage; be not afraid, neither be thou dismayed: for the LORD thy God is with thee whithersoever thou goest" (Josh. 1:9).

IT'S ALL THE WAY

I believe there is a spiritual moment in every believer's heart when he or she simply crosses over the line, determined to go all the way with God. It is not necessarily an emotional thing, which can sometimes be conjured up with music or eloquent preaching, only to be forgotten soon after. Rather, it is a decision that affects the rest of your life. It is the decision that simply says yes to God. "I am going with God, whatever that means. I am not drawing back. By the grace of God, I am not going to quit when it gets hard. I am going to trust God for the power to finish this journey."

It all starts with getting out of where you shouldn't be—by putting away known sin. You are not going to walk into where you should be until you get out of where you shouldn't be. If you need to get out of some lifestyle or practice that you know is wrong, I urge you to make that decision today. If you are living in sin, get out now; get out quickly! You are in a dangerous place if you begin to call evil good in the sight of God. Don't fall into the religious trap of becoming your own god and justifying wrong.

Perhaps lately you have been under conviction—you have been reading your Bible and the Holy Spirit has had His finger very clearly on an area of your life. If this is the case, do not put off obedience, for if you do, you will likely end up making peace with your sin. You will cover it and call it holy, as is the habit of the fallen nature of the human heart. Instead, make the choice today to say, "I will not justify wrong, I will not call indifference holy, I will not call selfishness godly. I am out of here; I am going with Jesus!"

WITH ALL YOUR HEART

Choosing to follow God all the way means a determination to believe His Word with all your heart. Without a heart of faith, you will be forever learning but never coming to the knowledge of the truth. You will accumulate Bible knowledge and even quote verses; but like Martha of Bethany, when Jesus comes to do the miraculous, all you will be able to do is quote Scripture without truly understanding it or personally believing it.

Unfortunately, many people end up just like the children of Israel—wandering in the wilderness. There is a personal wilderness that we all go through at some point in our lives—the place where we are tempted and tried, just as we saw Jesus experienced. But there is also a type of wilderness where you are neither going back to where you came from nor going forward to where you should be. How many people live like that in the house of God— in a place where they are basically going nowhere? They cannot truly say on Friday that they are not like they were on Monday. They cannot get up in the morning and rejoice, saying, "Oh, God, I see new mercies every day! I am changing by the Spirit of God into who You have created me to be." The wilderness is an awful place to be.

It was an "evil heart of unbelief, in departing from the living God" (Heb. 3:12) that kept the children of Israel in the wilderness, and they serve as an example and warning for us today. The bottom line is that the half-hearted are not going to make it. Those who refuse to embrace God's Word with all of their heart will end up turning to a false Christ in this last hour. It is only the heart of faith that gains the victory and pleases God; it is only the one determined not to stop short nor live in a halfway station between the past victories in Christ and the fullness of where God desires to bring His people.

STRETCH OUT YOUR HANDS

At one point when Jesus was with His disciples, He asked them who the people were saying He was. After the disciples gave Jesus various answers, ranging from John the Baptist to Jeremiah, He then asked them, "But whom say ye that I am?" Peter answered, "Thou art the Christ, the Son of the living God." Jesus replied, "Blessed art thou, Simon Barjona: for flesh and blood hath not revealed it unto thee, but my Father which is in heaven" (Matt. 16:15-17).

Peter was given a revelation from God, just as you and I have revelation from the Word of God and the Holy Spirit. If somebody were to ask us who Jesus is, we would proclaim that He is the Christ, the Son of God, and we would believe it just as Peter believed what he declared.

However, Peter did not realize the actual power behind the revelation until much later in his life, when he was willing to stretch forth his hands to the will of God. When Jesus appeared to His disciples after His resurrection, meeting them at the shore where they had been fishing all night without catching any fish, Peter was not yet walking in the fullness of power. Jesus said to him, "Verily, verily, I say unto thee, When thou wast young [a self-made man], thou girdest thyself, and walkedst whither thou wouldest: but when thou shalt be old, thou shalt stretch forth thy hands, and another shall gird thee, and carry thee whither thou wouldest not" (John 21:18). After Jesus spoke those words to Peter, He simply said to him, "Follow me."

We see here that choosing to follow God all the way means total abandonment to the kingdom of God—dying to your own will. It means stretching forth your hands and allowing God to lead you where you cannot go in your own strength and where most of us, if we are honest, do not want to go. Yet when Peter was willing to be led, he soon discovered that the power of God replaced fear. He went from denying Jesus before a servant girl and hiding behind closed doors with the other disciples for fear of the Jews, to boldly proclaiming the gospel and seeing God add thousands to the kingdom daily.

As you and I stretch forth our hands and abandon ourselves to God, He promises to provide us with all that we need for the journey—including freedom from fear: "The oath which he sware to our father Abraham, that he would grant unto us, that we being delivered out of the hand of our enemies might serve him without fear, in holiness and righteousness before him, all the days of our life" (Luke 1:73-75).

Although the Lord has given us many precious promises, He never promised that the journey would be easy. Jesus Himself spoke these words to His followers at the time: "Verily, verily, I say unto you, Except ye eat the flesh of the Son of man, and drink his blood, ye have no life in you. Whoso eateth my flesh, and drinketh my blood, hath eternal life; and I will raise him up at the last day. . . . As the living Father hath sent me, and I live by the Father: so he that eateth me, even he shall live by me" (John 6:53-54,57).

In other words, the life, the strength and the freedom we receive will not be our own but rather the very life of Christ flowing through us. However, that means not only must we be involved in the fullness of His redemption, but we must also be involved in the fullness of His redemptive work on the earth. We cannot just casually come to the things of God, decide to follow Him halfway, and then expect all of His promises and provision to follow. We must be fully given to His work on the earth. That means total surrender, total consumption, total giving of one's self, another life goal. A casual encounter with Christ or a mere form of religion will not give us the strength we need, nor will it bring freedom from fear.

After Jesus had spoken those words in John 6, we read that many of His disciples concluded that it was a hard saying and turned and walked away from Him (see John 6:60,66). We, too, must recognize that it is a serious decision to follow God all the way—to stretch forth our hands and be led, oftentimes away from our own will and desires.

There have been many times in my life when the Lord has asked me to lay things down, even things dear to my heart. For instance, when I reached my mid-50s, I began reflecting on how ever since I was a teenager I had spent my life working hard. More and more, I found myself thinking how nice it would be without the constant pressures that accompany being in the ministry—the demanding schedule, the spiritual battles. In my mind, I began to formulate an idyllic ending to my life. I would still do the things of God and perhaps speak at the occasional conference, but I would also have more time to rest and maybe even do some traveling.

I was on holiday recently enjoying time with my family, and once again I pictured how wonderful it would be to have more intimate time to spend with all of them, particularly my children and grandchildren. That is when the Lord reminded me of what He had once spoken to my heart: "Carter, all of your children are home, and you will have all of eternity to spend with them. But many of My children are not home yet. Help Me to get them."

The Lord had clearly asked me to lay down my vision of what my future should be like and follow the pathway that He had for my life. And so, I had made the decision to surrender these dreams to Him and go His way, no matter what the sacrifice. To this day, I have not regretted it.

THE HOUR IS COME

Perhaps you fear taking that necessary step of faith to be totally abandoned to the will of God. However, if you will have the courage to come before the Lord in honesty and bring Him all your fears, He will meet you right where you are and give you strength. What God is looking for is that desire to follow Him all the way, despite your frailties.

It all boils down to why you came to Jesus Christ in the first place. Was it merely to be saved from eternal peril, or was it because you truly had a desire to walk with God? Whatever the case, I encourage you not to settle for going halfway with Christ. It would be like having one foot in the boat and one on the dock. Tragically, many people never finish the journey because they simply cannot make the break from this world. But you and I must realize that we are leaving a perishing planet for a kingdom that is eternal. We have to make the break and want the whole thing—the full journey, abandoned to God and filled with His Spirit.

I urge you to make the decision now to follow God, for when the storm hits, it is a little late to try to get right with Him. Who knows how many people were putting off that decision in Noah's day, waiting for a more opportune time, completely unaware of how close they were to the end? Similarly, our world today is unraveling very quickly, and you must get oil for your lamp now. You are going to need strength to get through the coming days.

Jesus declared, "The hour is come, that the Son of man should be glorified" (John 12:23). Do you feel in your heart that the hour is come? It is not coming, it has already come! We do not have a million tomorrows. This is the hour that Christ is to be glorified in your home, in your city, in your country. This is the hour to make up your mind and settle in your heart that you are going to leave your fears behind and choose to follow God—all the way!

FEAR NOT

9

CHOOSE TO FACE YOUR ENEMIES

Thou comest to me with a sword, and with a spear, and with a shield: but I come to thee in the name of the LORD of hosts, the God of the armies of Israel, whom thou hast defied.

1 SAMUEL 17:45

When I was a young believer, the Lord began to tell me that He wanted to use my life for His glory. Now keep in mind that I was someone who was so fearful of being singled out in a classroom of 12 people that when it happened, I would run out of the room. Or if I didn't run from the room, I would panic from the knowledge that eventually the teacher's attention would focus on me. This meant that I was in danger of passing out, which actually happened to me a couple of times.

You may be asking, "Well, then, where did you start? Did you all of a sudden pop into a pulpit somewhere and miraculously start preaching to people without fear?" No! Do you know where it started? The Lord told me, "Stop running out of the room." So I did, and that is where it began. I heard the Lord continually reminding me to hold my ground.

YOUR ENEMIES ARE BEGINNING TO TREMBLE

In the days when the Philistines gathered to fight against Israel with 30,000 chariots, 6,000 horsemen and people as numerous as the sand on the seashore, King Saul and the men of Israel perceived that they were in danger and began to hide in caves and holes. The Scripture says that others followed Saul in Gilgal, trembling. Yet there was one who was not found among the fearful. Jonathan, son of Saul, turned to his armor bearer and said, "Come, and let us go over unto the garrison of these uncircumcised: it may be that the LORD will work for us: for there is no restraint to the LORD to save by many or by few" (1 Sam. 14:6).

Jonathan was not afraid to face his enemies, despite being accompanied by only his armor bearer. He understood that it was the Lord's battle, and so he confidently asserted, "The LORD hath delivered them into the hand of Israel" (v. 12). The two of them went forward, and the Philistines fell before them.

Jonathan and his armor bearer took only half an acre. It might have seemed like a small and insignificant victory, but when they claimed that half acre, it sent a shudder right through the ranks of hell. The Bible says that an earthquake and a great trembling went through the whole host. The Philistines trembled because finally somebody chose to believe God. They definitely did not regard this victory as insignificant.

Likewise, it was an incredible victory for me to stay in the room when I was filled with fear. I remember sitting there reminding myself, *God has not given me a spirit of fear, but of power and love and a sound mind* (see 2 Tim. 1:7). And so I would stand my ground. Then, from holding my ground in the room, invitations began to come to speak to small groups of people—a few here and there. I would actually take refuge in the bathroom before speaking to these small groups, so nervous to the point of feeling ill, but I would continue to remind myself of that same Scripture.

When I walked into these small gatherings, still feeling sick, I would assert in my heart, *I am not backing away from this battle.* Then I would start to speak, and the anointing would come every time. God would challenge people's lives, and they would be dumbfounded. You see, the battle is not ours, it is the Lord's! God said, "I will fill your mouth if you will just open it. I have put a river of living water in you if you will just begin to speak. I will speak through you and lives will be transformed" (see Ps. 81:10 and John 7:38).

I am not merely giving you another theory; I have lived this, and it has been an incredible journey. I have experienced the extraordinary power that God makes available if we choose to face our enemies and trust Him to carry us through.

YOUR ENEMIES ARE BREAD

When the 10 unbelieving spies brought back the evil report about the Promised Land, Joshua made a profound statement: "Only rebel not ye against the LORD, neither fear ye the people of the land; for they are bread for us: their defence is departed from them, and the LORD is with us: fear them not" (Num. 14:9). How strange to consider that all that opposes us—from within and without—could actually be bread for us! What exactly did Joshua mean, and how do we partake of this bread?

Let me show you an example from the New Testament. Consider the time when God used Peter and James to heal the lame beggar at the gate Beautiful. This incited the chief priests and elders, who had commanded Peter and John not to speak or teach at all in the name of Jesus. When they refused, the officials further threatened them.

Peter and John came back to the rest of the disciples and reported all that the elders and chief priests had said. What happened next? They all turned to prayer! Rather than shrink back in fear and become silent in the face of the enemy, they allowed the opposition's threats to ignite a prayer meeting! When they were told not to speak in the name of Jesus, they gathered in one accord to ask for more boldness to speak in the power of Jesus Christ! When the officials got upset that everyone was praising God for the miraculous healing of the lame beggar, the disciples asked God to stretch out His hand to allow even more miraculous signs and wonders to be done in the name of Jesus!

> And when they had prayed, the place was shaken where they were assembled together; and they were all filled with the Holy Ghost, and they spake the word of God with boldness. And the multitude of them that believed were of one heart and of one soul: neither said any of them that ought of the things which he possessed was his own; but they had all things common. And with great power gave the apostles witness of the resurrection of the Lord Jesus: and great grace was upon them all (Acts 4:31-33).

The place was shaken, the disciples were all filled with the Spirit of God and they held all things in common, which means they were moved to divine compassion. They were sustained with a fresh measure of boldness, power and grace—and it was all because of the enemies they faced without backing down. Their opposition had become bread for them!

Notice throughout the book of Judges that whenever the people dealt casually with God's promises and presence, an enemy would be raised. This would cause the Israelites to become fearful and try to find ways to survive; yet in the midst of it all, God's voice would come once again and say, "This is the way." Of course, God's way was always miraculous. Imagine 300 Israelites on a mountaintop with trumpets, torches and pitchers! In the natural, they were basically on a suicide mission, standing against more than 100,000 well-armed enemies and simply shouting, "The sword of the LORD, and of Gideon" (Judg. 7:18)! Foolishness to man, but to us it is the power of God!

Freedom from fear comes when you remember the reason for the opposition—when you remember that God has allowed it in your life in order to sustain and nurture you. When you choose to face your enemies, it is actually a key to unlocking the provision of God for your life and the lives of those around you.

Remember when the young lion came roaring against Samson as he went down to Timnah, and the Spirit of the Lord came upon him so that he ripped the lion with his bare hands? Samson returned that way later and found the carcass of the lion filled with honey, so he took some for himself and also for his parents. What was sent as a threat on his life and should have killed him turned out to be nourishment for himself and others (see Judg. 14:5-9).

Very often it is opposition that turns us to God. David said, "Thou preparest a table before me in the presence of mine enemies: thou anointest my head with oil; my cup runneth over" (Ps. 23:5). In the presence of our enemies! That is where God feeds us; that is where God pours out His anointing and supplies all that we need. Without opposition the Church gets lazy—she turns inward and seeks power without purpose, which is a formula for spiritual delusion. When the Church comes to a place where she is no longer opposed, she declines.

Perhaps you have been groaning in prayer for weeks, crying to the Lord, "Deliver me from this!" But you must realize that when you pray this, you are actually saying, "Oh, God, remove the bread from the cupboard; take the drinks out of my refrigerator; take away my strength, my anointing, my cup!" If God were to give you everything you asked for, you would become a couch potato with a Bible on your lap. No, in His wisdom and love He is going to increase your enemies and cause you to turn to Him!

IT'S TIME TO GET UP

You have a choice to make now. You can sit on the hillside and listen to the voice of your condemner for the rest of your life and amount to nothing in God. "Oh, it's great that He did that for you. It's great that He did it in the book of Acts, but He will never do it for me. My enemies are too big, and I am too weak." You may even continue to go to Bible studies, study about God and polish your armor until you can see your reflection in it.

Or you can stand up and recognize the purpose of the opposition in your life. You can choose to believe that as you turn to God, He will give you courage to face your enemies and triumph over them. Even if you have no more than just one promise from the Word of God, it is time to get up and go into the valley to face your giant, saying, "You are not defying me, you are defying the God who created this universe. He has interwoven the very honor of His name in keeping and sustaining me, in using my life for His glory. You are defying the God who bought me with His blood 2,000 years ago!"

David defeated the most fearsome enemy pitted against the people of God in his generation, and all it took was one stone, not a gravel truck. It was like coming against the enemy with one promise, one victory that he had already seen in his life—perhaps insignificant in the sight of man, but great in the sight of God. You do not need to use a hundred Scripture verses, you just need to believe what you read. And just as the Philistine army must have laughed at the sight of David running toward

Goliath with a sling and a stone, people today who are guided by human reasoning and human effort will regard it as insanity to fight with this kind of weaponry. Little do they know of the simplicity of the power of God that comes upon a heart of faith.

I have always felt it is better to die for the glory of God than to live as a coward. We need people who are going to stand up in this generation—in the business world, in the entertainment world, in every neighborhood, in every home. The Lord deserves to have a body of believers in this hour who will take Him at His word and face their enemies—who will not be content to sit around and do nothing as the devil devours young people in the streets, shatters marriages and destroys families. There should be irrefutable evidence in His people that there is a God to be reckoned with, who triumphs over our enemies. The Scripture clearly says that the Church age is to be a compelling testimony—that those around us must be confronted with the reality that Christ is alive and sits at the right hand of all power.

Just as Joshua told the people not to turn back in fear, so too the Lord reminds you today: Your enemies are bread for you; their defense has departed from them. Without the lion, without the bear, without Goliath, there was no bread. So do not fear, for without the enemies, you would never understand the power or the provision of God. Your enemies are feeding you, sending you to a place of nourishment and strength in God. They could not come against you unless God allowed it.

Choose this day to face your enemies. Rather than retreating in fear, ask God for spiritual eyes to see what you are actually facing. Will you see giants in the land, or will you see as God sees? Let the opposition drive you into the prayer closet—straight into the presence of God—and then you will be able to face all your enemies in the power of your God.

FEAR NOT

10

CHOOSE TO LOVE

There is no fear in love; but perfect love
casteth out fear: because fear hath torment.
He that feareth is not made perfect in love.

1 JOHN 4:18

Here is how I believe God is going to keep us from fear: He is going to bring us to the full understanding that He loves us with a perfect love—a love that belongs only to God and to those with whom He chooses to share it. When our faith is in Jesus, we are loved and fully received by God as if we had never sinned in our entire life. Even if we have had the worst week of our life, God still loves us with a perfect love.

"We love him, because he first loved us" (1 John 4:19). God loved us before we even knew or cared that He was there. When you were out in the clubs; when you were stealing, lying, cursing, gambling; and even when you were violent, He loved you with a perfect love! "The LORD hath appeared of old unto me, saying, Yea, I have loved thee with an everlasting love: therefore with lovingkindness have I drawn thee" (Jer. 31:3). In other words, God draws us to Himself because He wants to be kind to us—it is His desire to show us mercy. Not because we loved Him, but because He loved us first.

LOVE THAT RUNS TO US

God's love brings incredible hope and change. In Luke 15, we are given one of the purest and most graphic illustrations of the love of God in the entire New Testament, aside from the cross of Jesus Christ. Within these lines of Scripture, God describes His unconditional love for every son and daughter.

> A certain man had two sons: and the younger of them said to his father, Father, give me the portion of goods that falleth to me. And he divided unto them his living. And not many days after the younger son gathered all together, and took his journey into a far country, and there wasted his substance with riotous living (Luke 15:11-13).

This son had made a mess of things and ended up very far away from his father, just as all of us have done at some point. He resorted to feeding pigs in a field, and for a Jewish boy, that was about as low as one could get. Pigs were considered unclean, the lowest creatures on the face of the earth, yet he came to the point where he was actually feeding them and allowing them to live. Similarly, many of us feed and are allowing unclean things to exist by our very actions. For instance, if people did not watch pornography, the pornographers would be out of business tomorrow.

One day, this boy got sick of the way he was living and decided to get up and go home. I believe it was his father's love that was drawing him. Perhaps the father was communicating with him once in a while—sending little messages about how good it was at home, how much food there was, how all the servants were. After all, how else did he know? He had been away for so long. Yet the Bible says that he came to his senses and said, "How many hired servants of my father's have bread enough and to spare, and I perish with hunger!" (Luke 15:17). Even when we are feeding things we should not be feeding, these messages of God's love keep coming to us—invitations to come home.

As the son made his way home, he found no condemnation. Instead, his father literally came running down the road to embrace him, just as our heavenly Father was waiting for us to come home. God sent Jesus down from heaven to earth because He loved us. A passionate love like this brings covering; it brings empowerment; it brings an invitation to join God on His journey of redemption throughout the earth.

I am overwhelmed daily at the incredible love of God. He is so infinitely "other" than we are—so much purer, so much holier, so much more intelligent. Yet He chooses to partner with us! How can we understand this love of God? It would be as if you or I found the most de-ranged, disadvantaged individual in town and said to him, "From this day forward, you and I are partners! We are going to walk together. If you ever need me, I will be there; if you need resources, I will provide for you. You can brag about me everywhere you go, and I will never deny you. If anyone should ask, I will tell them that we are brothers." Yet even that scenario would be closer than the bridge God made to come to us.

The cross was not a legal obligation on God's part; it was the love of God in its purest expression. He was not willing that any should perish; He was not willing to lose you. It does not matter how you have lived, where you have come from, your level of education or what you have been doing with your life. You must be convinced today that God loves you! He loves you with a love that sent Him to a cross to get you back. It is His love that brings the genuine believer out of fear and into an in-credible feeling of security about the future.

Jesus said, "My sheep hear my voice, and I know them, and they follow me: and I give unto them eternal life; and they shall never perish, neither shall any man pluck them out of my hand. My Father, which gave them me, is greater than all; and no man is able to pluck them out of my Father's hand. I and my Father are one" (John

10:27-30). We see that the full strength of God is committed to bringing you and me safely home. He seals us in the hand of God when we come to Christ.

Of course, He is talking about the genuine believer. Perhaps you are not the strongest; you are not without flaws or struggles, but you are an honest believer in Jesus Christ. Have you trusted in Christ for your salvation? Do you truly desire to walk with God? If you can honestly answer yes, He says to you, "Not only do I cover you, but I put you in my Father's hand. We are going to walk together through flood and through fire, and one day I am going to open my hand and drop you at the throne of almighty God in heaven. We will have walked this journey together, and you will realize it was the love of God that brought you through."

When we get to the throne of God, what do you think our song will be? What are we going to be talking about when we finally see the holiness of God, the absolute otherness of God—when we see the perfection of God's creation and fully understand what He did on the cross for us? "Thank You for loving me, Jesus!" That is all we will be able to say. "Thank You, God! My purest attempts at being holy in my own strength were only as filthy rags in Your sight. It has been Your love that has redeemed me, carried me and given me the power I needed!"

LOVE THAT CHASTENS

When you understand how purely and completely you are loved of God, another element of fear will dissipate—you will no longer be afraid of reproof. Your heart will be open to the correction of your Father as He sees you need it: "For whom the Lord loveth he chasteneth, and scourgeth every son whom he receiveth" (Heb. 12:6).

When you know you are loved, you are not afraid of the Bible or what the Lord may say. You are not afraid when He tells you, "I have something to say to you today. The way you are walking is going to hurt your future or the future of others." Honestly, I am more fearful of *not* knowing the Word, or not having the Lord examine my heart.

When the two disciples were walking on the road to Emmaus (see Luke 24), recall that although they knew the Word and had been in close proximity to Christ, seeing Him crucified had brought them to a place of hopelessness and fear. They were now on the verge of losing heart, a type of people that would say, "Lord, would You give me a word today?"

Some of you picked up this book with that very thought: "Oh, God, I need a word. You have to speak to me. I am afraid of the future; I am losing heart; I am losing hope. I don't even want to be alive in this generation. Please speak to me!"

What if the word Jesus has for you today is just like what He said to those disciples? "O fools, and slow of heart to believe all that the prophets have spoken" (Luke 24:25). In other words, "Oh, fool, slow of heart to believe that I died for you because I love you; that I am able to keep everything that is committed into My hand and bring you through every struggle and trial that you are ever going to face. Oh, slow of heart to believe that you are secure in My love!"

LOVE THAT KEEPS US

In these last days, I believe that we are going to have a deeper awareness of the love of God than we ever have before. We are going to settle the truth in our hearts that His love has the power to keep us. The devil has no right to condemn us or cause us to be afraid that our future is not secure.

What did the apostle Paul say? "I know whom I have believed, and am persuaded that he is able to keep that which I have committed unto him against that day" (2 Tim. 1:12). In other words, "I have given Him my heart, my life, my future—all that I have. He is going to keep me in this life and then take me home to be with Him." Paul did not need to be walking on a pathway of ease.

He did not understand everything, but he simply knew the God in whom he believed. He had a direct encounter with the love of God.

Perhaps such an incredible love may be difficult for you to receive today. You might be among those who say, "Lord, I am afraid to open up my heart to the fullness of Your love." You would feel much more comfortable if I had just pointed out the areas where you have failed and done wrong, for that is the image you have of yourself. Maybe somebody spoke such a word over your life at some point or told you that you were worthless. Perhaps the voice that you needed to hear was not there. You did not have a father or mother who could embrace you and say, "I am proud of you, son; I am proud of you, my daughter. I love you; I believe in you."

Maybe that was never in your life, and it produced a deep inner sense of unworthiness that makes it difficult for you to receive the love of God. But listen to what God says in the Song of Solomon, in the context of Christ speaking to His bride, His church: "Thou hast ravished my heart, my sister, my spouse; thou hast ravished my heart with one of thine eyes" (Song of Sol. 4:9). It happened when you merely looked toward Him! You did not even have a chance to fully turn toward

Him—it was only one look of your eye that caused Him to say, "The moment you looked toward Me, you stole My heart."

The Lord says, "I don't see you the way you see yourself. I have cleansed you, called you, empowered you, given My promises to you. You and I are going to walk together, not just through time but through all eternity, and it is going to be an amazing journey." The Bible does not say that perfect repentance casts out fear. Thank God for repentance, and of course it is a good and necessary thing. But it does not say that—it says, "Perfect *love* casteth out fear" (1 John 4:18, emphasis added).

LOVE THAT CASTS OUT FEAR

Yes, we will have a greater understanding of God's love, but how exactly will it manifest itself? I believe it will be through loving one another. As the Scripture says, "No man hath seen God at any time. If we love one another, God dwelleth in us, and his love is perfected in us" (1 John 4:12). Once we open our hearts to the love of God, we instinctively know that it also means we must open our hearts to other people. God puts His love for people in our heart, and it is this very love for others—love perfected, love matured—that casts out fear.

I am not talking about simply tolerating one another—about Sunday morning smiles. I am talking about absolutely loving one another in the power of God; seeing others as God sees them and caring as God cares. That means barriers must be broken down and the borders of our tents expanded to include other people, other races, other cultures, other classes. That means we have to choose to leave our comfort zone and allow God to stretch us so that we can be what He has called us to be.

It is this kind of perfected, mature love that casts out fear. Suddenly you will find yourself no longer afraid of the threats around you or the faces of the people. You will no longer be afraid of tomorrow, of being vulnerable, of giving, of failing to finish the course. You will not be afraid of stopping on the Jericho road and helping somebody who needs it. The fear will be gone. Instead, the love of God will be shed abroad in your heart!

The Lord has allowed me to experience this truth in my life. I once visited a maximum security prison that housed approximately 40 prisoners who were sentenced for life. Many of them literally lived to kill a policeman, so I understood the danger I put myself in when I told them I was an ex-cop. If they were to kill me, it really would not have made a difference—they were already in prison for life. But I wasn't afraid of them.

I told them plainly, "Listen, I'm not here because I have nothing else to do. I'm here because God has put compassion in my heart for you. You need to be forgiven just as much as I needed to be forgiven." I cannot fully explain what happened in that place, but all I know is that the Holy Spirit came. Soon, in the front of the room, there was a lineup of men receiving Christ as their Lord and Savior. Men who were living lives full of hate suddenly found themselves crying because an ex-cop had led them to Christ.

I have traveled to war-torn areas of the world. I once stood on a platform and preached to several hundred Muslim men in a very volatile situation after the war in Kosovo. Yet I had no fear because there was a love in my heart for these men. They knew they were duty bound by some of their theological understanding to kill me, but we as a church had built a bridge for them, so they were culturally bound to be hospitable. I spoke to them that day about the love of God, and many in that crowd began openly weeping. These men in their thirties and forties, who had just fought a war, were wiping their faces because the love of God had touched their hearts.

I have stood in war zones in Africa. We were in Nigeria during a time when a curfew was in place because two people groups were at war with each other. On the first night of our crusade, an estimated half million people came out. We had been warned beforehand by many that this would be suicide for us. People were afraid that there would be an uprising—that the Islamic element would see us as the rallying point for Christians and would kill us. Yet I was not the least bit afraid.

All of this is not a false bravado; I share it with you as a demonstration of the truth that perfect love does indeed cast out fear. All these people were men and women created in the image of God, and I didn't really care what their perspective was at the moment. God created them, and they needed to know there is a Savior who went to a cross and died for them.

The Scripture says, "Herein is our love made perfect, that we may have boldness in the day of judgment: because as he is, so are we in this world" (1 John 4:17). As He is, so we are! As He loves, we are allowing Him to love through us. What He is doing, we are doing!

LET THIS BE YOUR FOCUS

You are going to have to love where He has placed you— the people of your city. And that love must begin in the house of God, in your heart and in mine. We are not going to win people with an argument; we are going to win them with the love of God in us. To be loved is the deepest cry of every person on this earth, and when that love of Christ finds an expression through your heart and mine, we will see a harvest like we never thought possible come to the house of the Lord.

Choose this day to open your heart to the love of God, and ask Him to show you how much He loves you. Instead of opening the Bible and being condemned all the time, let Him show you His love for you, and then let that love flow through you to others. It is a supernatural work that you cannot conjure up. It is something God must do, and that means He will have to take some of us through the valley of the shadow of death, for there is a resistance within each of us to fully receive and give love.

When you truly understand how much you are loved of God, and you allow this love to manifest itself in a love for other people, all fear of tomorrow will be gone. Let your theological focus be other people. You will be amazed how quickly you will grow in grace; how much the power of God will come into your life and change you.

I can honestly tell you that from the beginning of my walk with God, I have loved the Scriptures. I have studied the Bible and sat in some of the most profound conferences over the years. However, it was the love of God that changed my life. It was the love! There is no fear in love, but perfect love casts out fear. Let us choose to walk in this love of God all of our days—and then we will find true freedom from fear!

TIMES SQUARE ■ CHURCH

Visit Times Square Church at:

1657 Broadway
New York, New York 10019

(212) 541-6300

www.tscnyc.org

ARE YOU READY FOR
THE SHAKING?

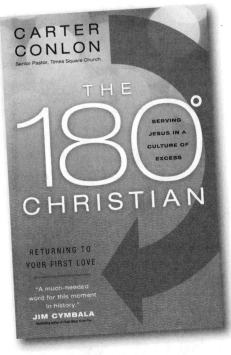

As our world grows ever dimmer, our society becomes increasingly jaded, and worldwide protests ensue for reasons far deeper than the demonstrators themselves can pinpoint, it's apparent that there is a universal cry of distress. Pastor Carter Conlon's question is: Will we as the followers of Christ make a difference?

This book has a word from the Lord for those who desire truth, strength and direction that promises to keep us strong in the coming days of shaking—that we may be sources of blessing and hope for others.

The 180° Christian
ISBN 978-0-8307-6095-4
ISBN 0-8307-6095-4

ALSO AVAILABLE

THE CLASSIC BESTSELLER FROM DAVID WILKERSON

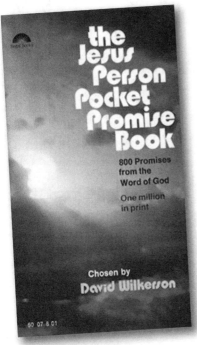

The Jesus Person Pocket Promise Book contains 800 promises for the Word of God as selected by David Wilkerson (1931–2011), founding pastor of Times Square Church in New York. Each verse is categorized to speak to different situations that individuals face and will provide hope and strength to help you endure in whatever challenge you may be facing.

The Jesus Person Pocket Promise Book
ISBN 978-0-8307-0191-9
ISBN 0-8307-0191-5

MORE TITLES BY
CARTER CONLON

Quiet Times
Music CD

**Where Christmas
Never Ends**
Music CD

Day by Day
Music CD

**Clunky of
Maryborough**
Children's Book

**Katie & the Dogs
Are Gone**
Children's Book

**Every Good House
Needs a Mouse**
Children's Book

Petey Yikes!
Children's Book